BUILD YOUR WEALTH THROUGH PROPERTY INVESTMENTS

DISSECTING THE 8 MOST POPULAR TYPES OF UK PROPERTY INVESTMENT STRATEGIES.

CHARLES FLETCHER

CONTENTS

1.

2.

3.

4.

5.

6.

7.

8.

9.

INTRODUCTION

How would you like to get started investing in the UK property market? Since you've picked up this book, I'm going to assume that you've either dabbled in property previously, or are looking to get started and need an easily understood guide. There are many strategies you can use to make money with property in the UK. However, which ones should you use? Which ones are best suited for you and are they safe?

You'll find the answers to these questions and much more within these pages. The UK is set to experience a property boom like never before, despite what you might have read in the mainstream news. From 2020 to 2024, the value of the average property in the UK is expected to rise by 15% (Why should you invest in UK property?, 2021). The North West leads the way with an expected capital appreciation of 25%.

While the usual property hotbed of London has faced a glut of foreign absentee owners in the property market, the rest of the UK is relatively untapped. All of this means that there's a massive opportunity waiting for you. All you need to do is implement the right strategies and the money will take care of itself!

Of course, this is easier said than done. There are many nuances to property investing and it's easy to make mistakes. I ought to know! I've been in the UK property market for many years now. I've made mistakes that have embarrassed me and made me want to curl up into a ball and never emerge again! However, I'm still here—as are my properties.

Property investment gets complicated in a hurry if you focus too much on the jargon and neglect the underlying meanings of the terms and phrases you hear. In this book, I'm going to demystify all of this and give you a concise plan that you can easily adopt. Once you've read this book, you'll know exactly what you need to do next and how to do it.

I'd like to mention that property investing sounds easy on paper but there are many practical issues that arise. It's impossible for anyone to warn you of these in advance or give you a handy template to every issue out there. The most important tool that you can possess if you want to be a successful property investor is your mindset.

So what does this mindset look like?

The Mindset of Success

I'm not going to beat around the bush. You're going to face challenges like never before when you enter the property investment market. There are many investors out there and a few of them employ tactics that will leave you extremely dispirited. You might come away thinking that the only way to prosper is to use underhanded methods. However, this isn't true.

Your property investing experience is entirely in your hands. If that statement alarms you, don't worry, this is a very good thing. It means you're in full control of your success. There are many tasks that you need to master to be a successful property investor but none of them matter unless you have a mindset that pushes you to do what's necessary. That's what separates the ordinary from the extraordinary.

As you go about your journey, you'll find that your results might not go your way. You'll enter deals that seem great but have flaws within them. The average unsuccessful investor throws their hands up at this point and decides to do something else. A successful investor will dive in and find solutions to their issues.

A problem-solving mindset is what distinguishes a successful person from someone who doesn't make it. You need to assume that problems are a part of every deal you enter into, no matter how great it looks on the surface. Trust yourself to find solutions and to do whatever it takes to ensure you solve them.

There's a ton of opportunity out there, even in seemingly saturated markets. You'll be told that there's a lack of opportunity or that the economy is poor or that Brexit is going to crash the market and so on. These aren't true. The UK faces a chronic undersupply of housing and this drives prices higher relentlessly.

The BTL (you'll learn what this is shortly) market is worth one trillion pounds currently and, by some estimates, the number of renters in the UK are set to outstrip owners by 2039 (Why should you invest in UK property?, 2021). As demand grows, rental prices are bound to grow with it and, in some areas, you can earn as much as 12% returns on your investment.

If that's not an opportunity, I'm not sure what is! All you need to do is approach it with the right mindset and implement the right advice. So why is this book full of the right advice and why should you listen to me?

How I Will Help You

My property investing career began where I was born, in Surrey. As I mentioned earlier, I've made mistakes but more importantly, I learnt from them. These days, I live in London, an allegedly dead property center for domestic investors, and I own developments in the metropolitan area.

My reason for writing this book is simple: I love property and teaching people how to attain success through property investment. There isn't a single "right" strategy for anyone. The beauty of property investing is that you can implement any number of methods and achieve success. With success comes financial freedom.

After all, that's why we're in this, aren't we? The promise of financial freedom is a huge incentive for us to do whatever it takes to be successful. I'm here to help you along your path and show you how property investment can take you there. In this book, you're going to find details on the strategies that have helped me in the past.

You'll learn how you can make them work for you and the common pitfalls that you'll need to avoid. If you think you don't have enough money to make them work, think again. I'll show you how you can leverage a small amount of money to create a large amount of wealth.

So with all that being said, are you ready to dive into the world of property investing? Let's begin by looking at the BTL market.

1

SINGLE BUY-TO-LET

The easiest way for a beginner investor to get involved in the UK property market is to invest in a single buy-to-let. Buy-to-let investments became briefly popular around 2006 to 2007 due to the way the housing market was structured back then. Many people opted to refinance their existing home's mortgage to purchase buy-to-let properties that boosted their net worth.

The problem was that the refinance rates they opted for were teaser rates. Once the real rates kicked in, they couldn't afford payments and lost their properties. This gave buy-to-lets a bit of a bad reputation. However, it wasn't a property characteristic that made them poor investments. It was the way investors structured their deals that made all the difference.

These days, the housing market is much different and you won't find the same kinds of financing offers that existed a while ago. However, there are many nuances of buy-to-lets that you must be aware of.

WHAT ARE THEY?

So what is a buy-to-let? A buy-to-let property is ready to be rented and you can earn cash flow from it immediately as an investor. You don't need to upgrade it a lot or sink too much money into it to spruce it up. In America, these properties are called turnkey rentals and you might find a few properties in the UK advertised as such.

Whatever the name, the point of a buy-to-let property is that it's ready for an investor to lease to renters and earn returns. What kinds of returns can you earn? This depends on the kind of deal you set up for yourself. On average, you can expect around five percent to six percent rental yields in the United Kingdom. Keep in mind that this is the average yield.

In places like London, you'll find yields around four percent to five percent. In the Northern counties, you can expect higher yields. The yield you can expect from a property is one of the most basic indicators of profit. Let's examine this in more detail.

Yields And Other Measures of Profit

Calculating the rental or gross yield is simple. You divide the annual rent earned by the property price. For example, if you paid 100,000 pounds to purchase a property and earn 5,000 pounds from it every year, your gross yield is (5000/100000) five percent. Many investors seek to maximize the gross yield in their properties.

A famous investing rule that involves the gross yield is the one percent rule. This rule states that the monthly rent you earn from a property must be one percent of the property's overall value. From the previous example, this means your monthly rent must be one percent of 100,000 pounds which is 1,000 pounds. The annual rent will be (1000*12) 12,000 pounds.

Why should you look to maximize your gross yield? The simple answer is that you'll incur expenses when you manage the property. You'll have to pay for maintenance and will be accountable for taxes. These chip away at your returns and the amount of free cash you can pocket will be lower than what the gross yield suggests.

The amount of free cash you can earn from a property is calculated by subtracting all the costs of running and maintaining the property from the monthly rent. Multiply this number by 12 to get the annual costs. Divide this annual number by the property's value and you'll have the capitalization rate or cap rate. Here's an example:

> Property value = 100,000 pounds
> Monthly rent = 1,000 pounds
> Yearly rent = 12,000 pounds
> Monthly costs = 500 pounds
> Yearly costs = 500*12 = 6,000 pounds
> Net Operating Income or NOI = 12,000 - 6,000 = 6,000 pounds
> Capitalization or cap rate = NOI/Property value = 6000/100000 = 6%

The cap rate is also called the net rental yield since it takes all of the expenses incurred into account. In the interest of establishing standards, a net yield or cap rate between four percent to six percent is excellent. Remember, your wealth also increases as the price of the property increases. Cash flow isn't the only way you'll earn money.

The yield you receive from a property depends on many factors. Let's take a look at some of them.

Location

Location is the most important factor when it comes to real estate investing. There isn't one type of location that guarantees investing success. The type of location you choose needs to be married to your investment strategy. When it comes to buy-to-lets, you need to choose locations that are suitable for the kind of person who will rent your property.

For example, if you've purchased a two bedroom unit, you'll need to make sure the location is close to good schools and is family friendly. After all, you'd expect a young family to move into your property. They'll probably have kids or be expecting them. The location has to be safe and the crime rates need to be low.

The presence of good employers in the area also boosts the value of the property at that location. Note that it's better to choose a location that offers access to several employers as opposed to one or two. If those businesses suffer, the value of your property will sink along with them. You need to limit your risk as much as possible.

The location's prestige also plays an important role. For example, properties in London will attract greater valuations and more price appreciation. By some estimates you can expect five percent yields in London with price appreciation of 16% (Where to invest in a buy-to-let property to get the best return, 2021). In contrast, properties in Yorkshire and Humberside attract close to seven percent in yields but just five percent in price appreciation.

It's important that you take the full picture into account before choosing a property. Some buy-to-lets will offer greater yields while others will offer greater price appreciation. The ones offering the latter won't put cash into your pocket as the former will. If this is in line with what you want, then choose the latter.

Tenant Quality

Many first-time landlords and property investors neglect to take the quality of their tenants into account when putting their properties to let. The quality of your tenants will determine how steady your cash flow will be and how much you'll need to spend on maintenance. Most importantly, it'll also help you to minimize the amount of time your property will lie vacant.

When considering the costs that a landlord faces, maintenance and emergency repairs occupy the top of the list. Very few take vacancy costs into account. Your property is unlikely to be occupied every day of the year. Your goal as a landlord should be to have it occupied as much as possible. There are two ways you can do this.

The first is to choose stable tenants who are more likely than not to occupy your place. The second is to not care about the quality of your tenants and back yourself to market your property effectively to find a steady stream of tenants. Needless to say, the first option is far more attractive and requires less effort.

A good tenant is more likely to pay you rent on time and will maintain your property well. They'll reduce your maintenance costs and you won't have to worry about them making loud noises at inconvenient times. After all, you cannot continue to house people who are a nuisance to their neighbors.

Your choice of property plays a big role in determining the stability that you experience with your tenants. For example, a one bedroom flat might attract great tenants. However, the nature of the property means they'll eventually move on to a bigger place. Contrast this with a two bedroom, detached bungalow that has a nice garden in a suburb.

The tenants who will be attracted to this property will likely be a young family who will stay in place for at least five years or so. If they have young children, you can bet that they'll do their best to maintain a stable housing situation as much as possible. This means that you, as the landlord, get to collect rent for more than a decade.

So make your life easier and choose properties that attract stable tenants who will treat your place as if it's their own. Create a list of qualities you want in a tenant and screen all applicants for them. Have your tenants jump through small hoops to screen out the ones who are unreliable. You'd be surprised how effective a simple application form is in clearing out the applicants who want to pay you in cash and have unreliable sources of income.

Transport Links And Infrastructure

How well is the location connected? The greater the number of road, rail, and air links in an area, the better the prospects are for property price appreciation. More people will move into the area because of the good transport options and you'll attract stable tenants.

If you're feeling adventurous, you can buy property in future commuter hotspots. As time moves on, certain areas come into vogue and buying property in these places ahead of time is often a good move. This especially applies to London's commuter belt. As the city grows, more areas will appear as hotspots for people to commute into the city.

Mobile And Broadband Connectivity

As little as a decade ago, this wasn't much of a factor. However, these days, it's extremely important. If you're living in a rural area, access to broadband internet is one of the first factors you should look at. People are increasingly online these days and a location with poor internet is far worse than one with no internet.

Take note of the local council's attitude towards broadband coverage being expanded. Many councils oppose the erection of masts and signal towers and this has led to many areas having no access to high-speed internet. Whatever the councils' argument might be, there's no doubt that their stance will have a negative effect on the desirability of your property.

Schools

School catchment areas have higher property prices on average than areas that don't have one. This means you should pay attention to the OFSTED report about a school. It's best to look for schools whose OFSTED reports are improving, although this doesn't have to be a priority.

Simply look for areas that have desirable schools within them and search for property there.

Quality of Life

This is a qualitative factor and many things go into determining the quality of life in a location. The quality of life a neighborhood has to offer depends on the tenant mix in that neighborhood. For example, a neighborhood with a younger demographic will favor nightlife options and the presence of entertainment options nearby.

An older demographic will favor space, access to quality healthcare, and the presence of good schools. The best way to figure out the quality of life a place has to offer is to look at the list of qualities you desire in a tenant and ask yourself whether they'd like to live there.

Often, local councils will offer landlords incentives to buy property in an area. While these incentives are great, most of these neighborhoods need some refurbishment, for lack of a better word. After all, the council of a highly desirable area is unlikely to need incentives to attract buyers.

Don't make incentives the only reason to invest in a property. Take all of the other factors into account before you make a decision. Every once in a while, you'll see a neighborhood undergo gentrification through these incentives. These opportunities are excellent ones to take advantage of. Look for empty high street shops and static or declining property values in such neighborhoods.

These sound counterintuitive but the presence of incentives along with these telltale signs of bad neighborhoods indicates that the council is heavily investing to improve the neighborhood. You could earn a windfall if you plan your purchase right. Another great sign is the presence of a ton of scaffolding in the area.

The presence of scaffolding might indicate that everything's about to fall apart. However, the reality is that owners in the area probably recognize the improvements that are about to occur and are taking the time to spruce up their properties' curb appeal.

Property refurbishment also indicates that the existing owners might be looking to resell for a higher price. All of these are great indicators to you as an investor. Note that properties in such areas will likely need some refurbishment and sourcing a true buy-to-let might be difficult. If you buy a refurbished property, your rental yields aren't going to be very high and you might be better off sticking to a neighborhood that doesn't need upgrading.

Quality of Retail Outlets

A good sign of a desirable neighborhood is the presence of cool retail outlets, such as Starbucks, Costa Coffee, and Waitrose. Waitrose, especially, is a great indicator of an affluent neighborhood and research has shown that the presence of a nearby Waitrose boosts property values (Anatomy of a property hotspot - 12 indicators, 2021). The presence of retail parks and shopping centers is also a good sign of a neighborhood that has some money to spend.

Ideally, you'll want to get in before these developments take place. However, buying properties with existing outlets within their neighborhoods is also a good option. The presence of these outlets don't necessarily indicate the presence of great tenants. However, you can rest assured that the people in that area are financially stable.

SOURCING YOUR BUY-TO-LET

Sourcing eligible properties is much easier than you think. The hard part is determining what kinds of properties you want to invest in. Many investors rush right in and buy the first thing that comes up. However, this approach is unlikely to yield good results. I mean yield in a literal sense.

Many properties are advertised as having high yields on their listings but, when you dig further, you'll discover that the listing agent has been taking a few liberties. Here's a step-by-step process that will help you to locate the best deals out there.

Start Close to Home

There's no better place to begin than the neighborhood in which you're currently living. You know it and the financials of the neighborhood well. Even if you don't know these numbers, you can always ask around and people are more likely to share this information with you since you live there.

Let everyone close to you know that you're looking for good properties to invest in. Choosing to invest locally also removes the question of property type from your list of things to decide. More likely than not, the property you invest in will be similar to the one you're currently occupying.

If these kinds of properties aren't your first choice, then expand your area of research to neighboring places. Often neighborhoods that are close to one another will have different property types and you'll find something you like close to where you live.

You can use listing sites, such as Rightmove and Zoopla, to research properties close to you. Another good move that you can make is to speak to estate agents in your area. Let them know what you're looking for and develop a working relationship with them. Estate agents can help you to land deals before they hit the open market.

Research Statistics

There are a few numbers to keep in mind when researching buy-to-lets. Since you won't be investing any money, or not too much money, into upgrading the property, you'll want to ensure that it begins paying you rent as quickly as possible.

Use the factors I previously listed to figure out whether a property is a good investment or not.

The most important figure to pay attention to is the rental yield. Anything greater than five percent is considered great in the UK. Finding properties that adhere to the one percent rule within the buy-to-let space is tough, so stick to looking for properties that yield you above average returns.

Once you've located a property you'd like to purchase, it's time to finance the property.

Arrange Financing

Unless you happen to have cash lying around, you'll have to finance your buy-to-let. A buy-to-let mortgage is a very different beast from a regular mortgage. The amount of rental income that you can expect to earn from the property determines how much you can borrow. Many lenders have limits based on rental income.

As a rule of thumb, most lenders require your monthly rental income to be at least 25% greater than your monthly mortgage payment. There are a few moving parts to a buy-to-let mortgage. The first cost associated with them is the product cost. This cost is fixed and you'll either pay a fee or the bank may waive this charge. Note that if they waive this charge, they'll charge you somewhere else.

The second cost to note is the term of the mortgage. This is usually 25 years. If you don't see a term mentioned, you can assume this is the case. Do not confuse the term of the mortgage for the fixed term length. For example, you'll often see loans named as “1.8% Buy-to-Let 2 Year fixed (Purchase only)” The “2 Year” portion indicates that you’ll pay 1.8% interest per year for two years.

Once the two years elapse, you’ll pay what is called the APRC or annual percentage rate change for the rest of the mortgage’s term. This rate will be listed separately. The APRC is also referred to as the follow-on rate. Your monthly payments will rise once the initial fixed period elapses. Make sure that you budget based on the higher interest rate, not the lower fixed one.

Buy-to-Let, or BTL, mortgages require you to deposit 25% of the property's value upfront. This is considerably more than what you would deposit with a regular mortgage. Also, you’ll have to pay the stamp duty land tax which is greater on a BTL than a regular purchase.

You’ll need to apply at a local bank to get final terms. You’ll have to produce income proofs and other asset proofs. As much as possible, opt for a fixed rate loan. However, a fixed rate loan will make it harder for you to qualify for the mortgage payment to rental income threshold. Many investors opt for an interest only, variable rate loan.

Their reason for this has to do with their exit strategy.

Figure Out Your Exit

Many BTL investors don’t take the time to figure out what they’ll do with the property. They don’t go beyond the fact that they’ll place it on rent and earn some cash. How you plan on disposing the property (or not) dictates the kind of loan you'll opt for. Fixed rate loans are the least risky but they come with the greatest interest rates, often as high as five percent. This means that very few properties qualify for the threshold I mentioned previously.

To qualify for the threshold, investors opt for variable rate loans. The interest rate on these loans fluctuate according to the Bank of England base rate or the BEBR. Currently, the BEBR is at record lows but, over the next decade, you can expect this rate to rise. As the rate rises, your monthly payment rises along with it.

To mitigate this rise in payment, investors can opt for interest only loans. In these loans, your monthly payment will go towards paying off the interest on the loan, not the principal. This means that you'll owe the amount you borrowed at the end of the loan term. The flip side is that your monthly payments will be far lower than on principal and interest payment loans.

However, the balloon payment at the end puts considerable stress on investors. To avoid having to come up with a ton of cash at once, many interest only borrowers plan to sell their property before the end of the loan's term. This way, they'll cash in on the rise in home value, earn higher than normal rental yields, and pay the bank at the end of the term. Sounds good on paper.

Truth be told, it's a great strategy but it's an extremely risky one. Do not opt for an interest only variable rate loan if you don't have a clear vision of how you plan on exiting. Remember that the market could change over time and you might not be able to sell your property when the time comes. If you can't make your balloon payment, the bank will seize your property and your credit score will nosedive.

Find Tenants

If you've selected your property well, you shouldn't have too much problem attracting tenant inquiries. The challenge is to screen these tenants for the right ones. You can advertise your property to-let situation in the neighborhood, through people in your network, websites, such as Craigslist, through local estate agents, and national websites, such as Zoopla and Rightmove. Note that these websites will charge you a listing fee, much like how an estate agent will charge you a commission for finding tenants.

Make sure that you have every prospective tenant fill out an application form and run a credit check. Make sure that you receive permissions from the tenant to run a check in writing and have them sign it clearly. Many first-time landlords have trouble organizing property viewings, especially if they have a full-time job.

The best way to handle multiple viewings is to assign a block of time during the week and inform everyone that they can view the space then. Do not encourage viewings outside this block, or else you'll have no time for yourself. For example, you could inform applicants that they can view your property on Saturday between two to six in the evening.

Creating these hurdles weeds out the people that aren't serious or don't have documented sources of income. Once you locate your ideal tenant, have a solicitor create an agreement for you and use that as a template in the future. Specify when your tenants can move in and the terms by which they can lease your property. Collect the rent and the security deposit and you're all set!

Maintain

Preventive maintenance will save you a ton of money down the road. Many landlords carry out maintenance only when something breaks. This is costly and will only drive away good tenants. Make sure you inspect pipes, electrical connections, and general structural integrity once every month.

Carrying out preventive fixes beforehand will let your tenant know that you're serious about property upkeep and that they can rely on you to fix any issues. This ensures that they'll stay with you for longer.

ADVANTAGES OF BUYING TO LET

So what are the advantages of buy-to-let investing? As you've already seen, the process isn't terribly complicated, aside from following a few simple rules of thumb. While you won't be investing in below market bargains, there are a few advantages of this investment method.

Boost to Long-Term Net Worth

Once you assume control of a property, your net worth receives an instant boost. This is because the market value of the property is added to your net worth. You can use this increased net worth to finance other deals you might have in mind. Part of the reason why this happens is because property prices almost always increase over time.

The capital gains of purchasing property can be significant. Even with buy-to-let properties where you aren't purchasing properties for a bargain, you can expect value increases of at least two to five percent every year. Of course, this is an average number that applies to the UK as a whole. Your individual gains might be lower or greater than this figure.

Either way, as long as you're buying a property at sensible prices, you can expect your wealth to grow over the long-term considerably. The rent that you'll earn over time will also boost your overall returns, giving you two ways of earning money.

Deal Structure

When you purchase a buy-to-let, you can use the property in any way you please. One of the biggest advantages is that you can have the rent cover your mortgage payment. In effect, you'll get paid to own the property. I must mention that your rent won't always cover your mortgage in all areas. In the London Metropolitan area, for example, you can expect the rent you earn to cover around 70% of your mortgage payment.

However, compared to a homeowner in that area who pays a full mortgage, you'll get to own the same property for a fraction of their cost. In some areas, especially in the North, you can have some money leftover from your rental payments after the mortgage is covered. In effect, you'll earn money to hold onto the property for as long as possible.

The prevalence of interest only loans also changes the picture. With interest-only mortgage payments, you can earn even more money every month and funnel that into other deals you might want to make. The result is faster compounding of your wealth. You can use the cash flow from one property to pay for the deposit of another and so on. Granted, this is a risky strategy since you'll be assuming a lot of debt and will be liable for balloon payments at the end of the mortgage term. However, if you can pull it off, it'll boost your wealth considerably.

Even if you don't want to place your property to let, you can use it as a second home. Place it to let on Airbnb or any other website when you aren't occupying it and use it when you please.

Tax Benefits

As a homeowner, you can offset property-related expenses against your tax bills. Over the past few years, property taxation has changed considerably and this has pushed a few buy-to-let owners into the red. You'll read a lot of negative information about how buy-to-let investing isn't tax friendly anymore. This isn't the case.

Previously, landlords could deduct their entire interest expense from their taxes. If you drew an interest-only loan on your property, this meant the entire mortgage payment could be offset against your taxes. As a result, the entire rental payment was yours to keep. You can imagine the windfalls that landlords realized.

However, these days, you can receive a 20% tax credit on your finance costs. In effect, 20% of your interest is paid for by the government. In addition to this, you can also deduct the following expenses (Landlord tax changes: What are allowable expenses?, 2021):

- General maintenance and repair costs
- Water rates, council tax and gas and electricity bills (if paid by you as the landlord)
- Insurance (landlords' policies for buildings, contents, etc.)
- Cost of services, e.g. cleaners, gardeners, ground rent
- Agency and property management fees

These expenses will greatly reduce your tax bill and boost your income earned from the property.

DISADVANTAGES

It isn't all advantages when it comes to buy-to-let. There are a few disadvantages that you should be aware of as well. Here they are, in no particular order.

Stamp Duty

When you buy a property, or finish arranging financing on it and are ready to take possession, you'll need to pay three percent stamp duty charges. This amount is calculated on the cost of the property, not just your deposit. For example, if you purchase a 100,000 pound property, you'll owe 3,000 pounds in stamp charges.

Many landlords don't take this payment into account and find themselves short of cash when the time comes to close the financing so prepare in advance.

Tax Regulation

In recent years, the government has been making changes to tax regulations and this has made property investing tricky. It's impossible to predict what kind of changes will come next, so this is a significant risk factor. Having said that, it isn't as if you should avoid investing in property completely.

Instead, look to build a margin of safety within your deals. Instead of opting for interest only loans, pay the principal back as well. Look for deals where rents cover a good percentage of the mortgage payment and have some cash as backup for emergencies. Make sure that you have enough to pay your living expenses before investing in property.

By building a safety margin into your deals, you'll be prepared to weather any storms when they arrive.

Borrowing Difficulty

Despite the benchmark rate sitting close to zero, banks have been tightening lending requirements. This means finding financing, despite having impeccable credentials, is tough. You won't always be able to secure financing in a situation. There's no remedy to this, unfortunately. You'll just have to move on and find other situations that suit your needs.

Rental Voids

As I mentioned previously, most landlords automatically assume that their properties will always be occupied. This is almost never the case. No matter how well you screen your tenants, you'll have periods where your property will lie vacant. During these times, you'll have to pay the mortgage out of your pocket.

Many landlords don't take these periods into account when evaluating the finances of a deal. They assume they'll always have rents to cover mortgage payments. The result is they lose the property when they can't make mortgage payments. You can avoid this situation by assuming that you'll need to spend 50% of whatever you earn as rent on your property.

If you receive 500 pounds as rent, for example, automatically set aside 250 pounds in your bank account whether you incur any expenses or not. This will help you to build an emergency reserve for when the property lies vacant.

Depreciation

While the majority of property appreciates, there's no guarantee that it'll appreciate all the time. In some parts of the UK, property has depreciated and there's no way to predict what will happen in the future. You can mitigate the situation by choosing properties in locations that are likely to experience population growth over time.

Staying away from locations that are reliant on a single source of employment and areas that are currently overpriced are good ways of lowering your risk.

Legislation

Landlords have to comply with a number of rules and regulations. What's more, these rules change a lot. Ignorance is no excuse and you should keep yourself up to date with all of them. The best resource for landlords to keep pace with these regulations is the National Residential Landlord Association or NRLA. You can signup on their website at https://www.nrla.org.uk .

As you can see, there are a few things you need to consider when looking at a buy-to-let opportunity. While entering a situation isn't as straightforward as it might seem at first, this doesn't mean you should stay away from them. Do your research and locate properties in great locations using the guide that I've given you in this chapter. You'll find that buy-to-let opportunities are a great and almost hassle-free way of investing in property.

2

HOUSE IN MULTIPLE OCCUPATION

HMOs, or houses in multiple occupation, is a great strategy to use in the UK. It has a few advantages over a traditional buy-to-let situation. However, there are a few disadvantages as well, as you'll see in this chapter. So what is an HMO? If you've ever rented a flat and had flatmates in it, you've lived in an HMO.

Property experts define an HMO situation as one that has common areas with different living spaces contained in a single unit. For example, a bungalow that is shared between three people who occupy its bedrooms but share the kitchen and living areas is an HMO. So is a two bedroom flat where people occupy their respective bedrooms but share the common areas.

HMOs are extremely common living arrangements for young professionals and students. In the City of London, especially, HMOs are quite prevalent and are the go-to choice for any young professional who is in need of affordable housing close to their workplace.

As you can imagine, there's a lot of potential for people to abuse an HMO living situation. After all, what's to stop people from erecting a bunch of bunk beds in a bedroom and calling it an HMO while letting it out to six or more people?

To prevent these situations, councils mandate the need for an HMO license and specify a bunch of other regulations that landlords need to follow.

Before we dive into how you can invest in HMOs lucratively, it's important to look at why renters choose HMOs. Simply put, HMOs are a good way to source affordable housing. From the landlord's perspective, it increases the income generating capacity of their property. This means the yields that investors can expect from their properties are a lot higher than with buy-to-let properties. The average yield on an HMO is estimated at 6.3% (HMO property investment | Ultimate guide, 2018).

There are a few other advantages of HMOs that you'll learn later in this chapter. For now, understand that a quality HMO investment can do wonders for your investment portfolio while potentially reducing the traditional risks associated with property ownership.

IMPORTANT CONSIDERATIONS

Now that you know what an HMO is, it's time to look at some of the considerations you need to take into account before investing in these properties. Some of the considerations you learnt about in the previous chapter, such as location and tenant quality, apply here, as well. Indeed, those are universal requirements for good property investment.

With regards to HMOs, though, you have to adjust those requirements a bit since the kind of tenants you'll be looking for are different from those looking for a BTL property.

Location and Tenant Quality

With BTLs, the ideal location is a suburb that is well connected to a major metropolis or area of business. When looking at HMOs, you can include the metro area, itself, for investment opportunities. Some of the best HMOs tend to be in some of London's most popular areas, for example. This is because you'll be partitioning the property and letting out individual rooms to people.

The tenants you'll attract tend to fall into two categories. The first category is people who don't have too much disposable income. They might be looking to save money on accommodation or waiting to move onto a better location. The second category of people are young professionals who are well off but need to live close to their workplace for convenience's sake. Young financial professionals are a prime example of this type of renter.

Both categories of tenants contain desirable and undesirable people. For example, university students belong to the first category. You can divide the property to create more living space but if you rent your property to the wrong kinds of students, you might have to deal with a ton of property damage when they eventually move out. The flip side is that, by leasing to college kids, you'll always have a steady stream of demand.

For the first category of tenant, your ideal location will be close to college towns or within them. These locations must have excellent public transport since the average college student doesn't have space cash for a vehicle. You'll want to impose strict living standards in your lease agreement since this kind of renter tends to be "adventurous", for lack of a better word. Make sure you conduct regular preventive maintenance and inspections and don't hesitate to enforce the terms of your lease.

The great thing about renting to people in the first category is that you can partition existing space to create more living units. For example, a large master bedroom can be converted into two smaller living units. You'll have to pay attention to regulations and do everything within the law, needless to say. However, there are significant opportunities to boost rental yield.

With the second category of tenant, the closer your location is to central areas of interest, the better. Again, you'll need to enforce strict renting conditions in the lease. However, you can charge premium rental rates and, more often than not, your tenants will be willing to pay these prices.

You'll also find HMOs in areas that are a bit downtrodden. The tenants you'll attract in these areas will have financial trouble and you might find yourself leasing rooms to couples and families. While the financial ability of a tenant isn't a mark of their quality, you should exercise more caution in such areas since the quality of life tends to be worse.

The yields in these areas tend to be much higher than what you might earn with an average HMO. Don't go chasing yields. Make sure you fully understand the risks of being a landlord in a less-than-desirable neighborhood and act accordingly.

To sum up, location and tenant evaluation factors are a bit different from a BTL investment. Begin by looking at the kinds of people that rent HMOs and figure out where they prefer living. This will help you to narrow down appropriate opportunities.

Licensing

Something that you'll need to deal with as an HMO owner is the prospect of licensing. Many councils require landlords to register themselves as HMO operators before they can place their properties to let. Check with your local council for the registration requirements.

Typically, you'll have to demonstrate that your property fulfills the legal requirements of being classified as an HMO. The most important part of these regulations are bedroom sizes. The bedroom size for a single adult must be at least 6.51 square meters. This increases to 10.22 square meters for two adults. Children aged under 10 must be provided at least 4.64 square meters of living space.

When partitioning your property, make sure you adhere to these requirements. It's best to use the services of a contractor who has experience in making these changes and understands the regulations well. Don't try to cut corners here or else you might find your property being marked as irregular. You'll face legal trouble, not to mention losing rent during this period.

Time

One of the most important things to consider before investing in an HMO is the amount of time that you have to dedicate to managing the property. Given the partitioned nature of HMO property, you'll have to deal with multiple tenants, each of whom will need separate lease agreements with different term dates.

The increased number of tenants also increases the frequency with which you'll have to carry out maintenance and deal with "extra-curricular" circumstances. For example, two of your tenants may not get along with one another and this might be disrupting the third person's quality of life. One of your tenants might have a partner live-in with them during the middle of the lease period, and this might put you on the wrong side of regulations.

With HMOs, you'll have to deal with both small and large maintenance requests and this puts a heavy burden on your time. Most HMO investors have a manager look after their properties or hire a company to do this. The downside is that you'll have to pay them to do so. Property management companies usually charge 10% of your monthly rent as fees.

While they promise complete service, the fact is that you're another number in their book of business and it's unlikely they'll look after your property with as much care as you will. However, if you're short of time, feel free to use the services of these companies. Make sure you factor their costs when you run the numbers on the deal.

Deal Numbers

Whether you like it or not, maths is an important part of any deal. While you need to pay close attention to numbers in BTL deals, they're even more important in HMOs. This is because you can run into a number of unexpected situations with them. The good news is that applying the one percent rule is a bit easier with HMOs thanks to the higher yields they give you.

If you invest in properties that need refurbishment, your returns can be even higher. You can also invest in lease-ready HMOs but you should expect yields slightly below average with such opportunities. The ideal HMO is one that needs some refurbishment that will boost its market value and cash flow producing ability.

How much should you offer for these properties, though? A simple rule you can apply here is the 70% rule. Like the one percent rule, we have our friends from across the pond to thank for these nifty rules of thumb. The rule is quite simple. Subtract the cost of refurbishment and repairs from the after-repair value of the property and offer 70% or less of that number. Here's an example:

> After-repair value of property (estimated) = 150,000 pounds
> Cost of repairs = 8,000 pounds

Maximum offer price = 70% of (150000-8000) = 99,400 pounds

The lower your offer price is, the better your deal is. Begin negotiations well below this price and do not go above this number. This rule is a great way to account for unexpected repairs cropping up. It gives you a great margin of safety that you can apply and still clear a good amount of money on your deal.

Like with BTLs, it's helpful to estimate the costs of running your property at 50% of the total rentals when your property is fully occupied. Research rental listings in the area to arrive at the ideal rental price for your tenants. Always set aside some cash from this amount to tide you over during lean periods.

The great thing about HMOs is that you don't have to worry about rental voids as much as you do with BTLs. Despite the greater frequency of headaches that your tenants will create for you, you can rest assured that there are a large number of them seeking housing. Therefore, your properties are likely to be full more often than not. You should also use spareroom.co.uk to evaluate the rents you can earn from an HMO.

The other advantage of partitioning is that you can have the rent paid by a few tenants make up for the absence of one or two tenants in your property. This is something BTL investors don't have the luxury of leaning on.

When running the numbers on your deal, make sure that you take stamp duty and taxes into account. These numbers can throw your calculations off my a lot. Also, make sure that you can afford the mortgage payment in a worst case scenario where you aren't earning anything from your property. Always prepare for the worst and you'll find it easier to make money in your investments.

Relationships

Given the greater frequency of crises that you'll have to deal with whilst owning an HMO, the quality of your relationships within your network are the most important factor in your success. You need to be on good terms with handymen, plumbers, electricians, and other contractors who can help to maintain your property and keep it in good shape.

Before you invest in any property, meet with other HMO owners in your area and ask them about their experiences. While the overall experience a landlord has will be the same, there are subtleties to owning property in certain councils. Speaking to existing landlords will also help you to identify a good support network that you can rely on when a crisis hits.

Speak to local estate agents, as well. Aside from locating good properties for you, agents will also put you in touch with contractors you can rely on. Make sure that you identify a good support network before you close your deal. If you're searching classifieds for plumbers right when a pipe's burst in your properties, it's too late.

The kind of relationships you have will also help you to locate and source great deals before they hit the market. With

HMO investing, the true bargains are snapped up before they hit online listing sites or popular advertising channels. Speak to investors in the area, network with bank mortgage representatives, and estate agents. All of these people will keep an ear on the ground and help you to locate potentially good deals.

Starting with your local neighborhood is again the best choice. If your neighborhood isn't suitable, then expand your search. Online listing sites are great but remember that investing in far-flung properties is probably not a good move for a beginner investor. Unless you have extensive landlording experience, stick to HMOs that are close and aren't more than an hour's drive away.

This way you can respond quickly and take care of your tenants' needs before a problem gets worse. The more downtrodden your location is, the more attention you need to pay to the quality of your relationships.

Financing

As with every real estate purchase, financing is one of the most important parts of an HMO deal. What makes HMO financing tougher to understand is that each lender has their own requirements and it might seem as if there aren't any common standards. For starters, an HMO is a borderline commercial mortgage, which explains why lenders exercise a lot of discretion over the approval process.

Note that it isn't a commercial mortgage, though. Most lenders consider up to five or six living units as being an

HMO and, anything greater than that, a commercial property. The size of the unit also plays a role and is up to the lender's discretion. Generally speaking, it takes anywhere from four to six weeks for financing applications to be processed.

Like with BTLs, the rent you earn from the property is taken into account before providing terms. The quality and nature of tenants is also an important factor. Most lenders prefer lending to HMOs that appeal to student tenants or young professionals. If your property is an area that is likely to attract tenants on benefits, you'll have a harder time obtaining financing.

For such situations, I recommend using the services of a mortgage broker. You'll pay a few points extra in commissions but it's worth it if the deal is a good one. One of the key steps a lender takes prior to financing an HMO is valuing the property. Here's where landlords often get tripped up. Your lender will use normal surveying techniques and seek to take the value of other HMOs in the area into account.

If there aren't any comparable HMOs in the area, the unit is considered a single dwelling and is valued accordingly. So how does this impact you? Well, if you negotiate prices on the basis of it being an HMO with your seller, you might find that the bank will arrive at a different valuation and leave you out of pocket.

Therefore, always pay attention to the presence of other HMOs in the area and value the property at sensible prices. If there aren't any other HMOs, negotiate as if you're looking at a single property. In such cases, it doesn't make sense to talk about prospective rentals with the seller. I'll cover negotiation tactics in a later chapter in more detail.

For now, remember that you'll have to value the property sensibly for your deal's financing to make sense. In terms of the loan types you can choose, you'll have access to fixed and variable loans that can be interest only or principal plus interest. The advice I gave in the BTL chapter applies here as well.

As much as possible, opt for a fixed loan—even though this isn't always possible with an HMO. Don't go interest-only unless you know what your exit plan is and have a contingency plan in case it falls through. Mortgage rates on an HMO loan are comparable to those of a BTL. This is to say that they're higher than a regular mortgage. Typically, you'll receive rates for 75 LTV (25% deposit loans); however, the more you deposit, the better your terms will be.

Something else to take into account is the landlord criteria that a lender has. Some lenders stay away from first-time HMO owners or property owners. Generally speaking, if your first property investment is an HMO, your lender will specify that you must hire a property management company to handle day-to-day operations. Even experienced landlords might get hit with these requirements, especially if the interest rate on offer is attractive.

This means that, unlike BTLs, where you can browse online to get an estimate of the terms on offer, HMO mortgages are best shopped for in person. Often, using a broker smooths things out. Brokers have special relationships with lenders and can score better deals for you. Of course, you'll pay them a commission but, in the long run, it might be worth it. So shop around as much as possible and compare the rates you receive by yourself to the rates a broker obtains for you.

I must also mention that, if you're buying the HMO through a company, you'll need to demonstrate significant investing experience to qualify for financing. I'll cover the ins and outs of buying properties through companies in a later chapter but, for now, understand that, if you don't possess enough cash to forego financing or have enough experience running properties, buying an HMO through a company isn't a good deal.

Many investors open companies to buy property because they can write off interest payments as expense. As you've learned already, individuals can't do this. However, the decision to invest via a company or not is a complex one and mortgage interest write-offs should never be your only criteria.

ADVANTAGES AND DISADVANTAGES

By now, you should have a good idea of what the deal is with HMOs. Here's a quick recap of the advantages and disadvantages of investing in an HMO situation.

Greater Yield

The greater number of units in an HMO means that you stand to earn higher yields on your property compared to a BTL. You'll need to adhere to regulations when partitioning your property so make sure you use the services of a contractor who knows the rules. Before you apply for financing, have plans drawn up and rental revenue projections handy.

Yields on HMOs can be as much as four percent to five percent greater than on a comparable BTL. It's worth taking the time to dissect an HMO opportunity before you invest in one.

Responsibility

With greater yields, comes great responsibility. You'll have more tenants to handle and more issues to tackle. It's best to hire someone to manage the property for you since you'll need to devote considerable resources to ensuring your property is up to scratch. The upshot of this situation is that you're not going to have much time for a full-time job, unless you choose to outsource management entirely.

There are pros and cons of going down the management route. For one, you'll be another number in a portfolio for a management company. However, you can get some of your time back and won't have to worry about day-to-day management. It'll reduce your yield but you will get to collect cheques and not worry about anything else.

You'll also need to obtain licensing from the local council if you invest in an HMO. Each council is different so make a note of the fees you'll have to pay every year and factor them into your calculations.

Financing Process

The financing process in an HMO deal is a bit more involved than it is with BTL. Given it's borderline commercial nature, HMO mortgage applications are strictly scrutinized by lenders. Everything from the nature of the deal to the tenant quality to the owner's qualifications are examined for suitability.

As a result, there isn't a uniform standard across lenders. You'll need to shop around as much as possible before landing on a suitable financing option. It's best to use the services of a mortgage broker to ease the process. First-time landlords will find obtaining HMO financing more expensive than obtaining one on a BTL. You might be forced to hire a property management firm to comply with lending standards.

Demand

Unlike BTLs, where demand can ebb and flow, there's a near constant demand for HMO housing from the likes of students, young professionals, and people who are seeking cheaper housing. This means that you're unlikely to encounter rental voids and can rely on a steady stream of income despite higher tenant turnover.

Advertising costs are also low, thanks to a steady stream of tenants. All of this goes towards giving HMO landlords higher yields than their BTL counterparts.

To summarize, HMOs are a great opportunity but you need to thoroughly research the deal and make sure that the maths make sense. Don't rush into a deal just because the expected yield is high. Despite the transient nature of your tenants, you should not compromise on the quality of people to whom you lease your property. Make sure you have a good support network of professionals who can help you to maintain the property or hire a property management firm to make things easy for you.

3

RENT-TO-RENT

Rent-to-rent has become one of the most hotly debated ways of making money via property. Interestingly, it doesn't involve owning property. There are two camps of thought when it comes to rent-to-rents. The first camp thinks it's perfectly fine and is beneficial for landlords. The second camp, usually landlords, think it's a scam that their tenants try to play on them.

Here's how the process works on a high level. You rent a property from a landlord and then rent it to someone else. Sounds simple, doesn't it? Well, there are a few technicalities involved in the process. First, you need to negotiate a lower than market rate rental with your landlord. More often than not, they'll ask you to pay a sum in bulk to justify the discount.

This means you need to have cash to invest and can't rock up with a zero balance and expect to make large sums of cash. It doesn't work that way! You need to do your homework, much like any property investor would—and negotiate like one. The other side of the equation involves finding tenants and ensuring that the property is occupied as much as possible. You'll have to balance the landlord's expectations with your needs to turn a profit.

For example, you can't lease the apartment to just about anyone who turns up with a wad of cash. Your landlord can take you to court if they find that the tenant you leased the property to caused severe damage. I'll discuss the things to watch out for in more detail shortly. For now, don't fall into the trap of thinking rent-to-rents are a foolproof way of making money.

There's no doubt that the lower capital requirements mean they're more accessible. However, don't confuse accessibility for ease of operation. You'll have to do just as much work with a rent-to-rent as with a BTL or HMO. In fact, you'll have to work harder since you don't have the option of outsourcing management to a company.

After all, you're making money on the difference between what you paid the landlord and what you're receiving from the tenant. This differential will be a few percentage points on the rent you paid. For example, if you negotiated a rental payment of 500 pounds per month with a landlord, you can't realistically lease it out for more than 650 or 700 pounds, if you're lucky.

After all, you'll be dealing with seasoned landlords who know the market well. The key to success with rent-to-rents is volume. The more properties you have under management, the more money you'll make. In fact, the best way to think of a rent-to-rent investment is to think of yourself as signing a property management contract with the landlord. Except, you're guaranteeing rent to the landlord beforehand instead of simply managing it.

This means that you're adopting considerable risk. However, as you'll see, rent-to-rents are a great way to create cash flow without having to buy property.

WHY RENT-TO-RENT?

So why is this a great strategy? Aside from the low capital requirements, there are genuine benefits for the landlords you offer your services to. Let's take a look at some of these advantages now.

Cash Flow

One of the biggest headaches of owning property is generating adequate cash flow. The average landlord grows tired of finding tenants, screening them, maintaining the property, accounting for cash flow, and finding new tenants once the original ones move out. Landlording is a full time job and, over time, burns people out.

What landlords love more than anything else is for someone to come in and relieve their stress. If you can come in and assure them of cash flow, which is what every landlord wants from their properties at the end of the day, they'll be more than willing to give you a discount. Of course, cash flow isn't the only criterion that a landlord evaluates when striking a deal with you.

Landlords don't expect experienced investors to approach them for rent-to-rent opportunities but you need to display the ability to run the property without supervision. After all, the landlord is taking a risk by allowing you to source tenants for them and maintain the property. If you set unrealistic rents and fail to market the property, they stand to lose as well.

So always do your homework on the property rents in the area and understand what the landlord is looking for. They have a built-in incentive to offer you a good deal but you need to show them that you're worthy of it.

No Financing

The biggest hurdle that beginner property investors face is money. To invest in property, you need to pay a deposit to finance your purchase. Unless you have heaps of cash lying around, you'll have to go through the financing application process and stump up cash to deposit. Usually, this is 25% of the property's value.

The deposit isn't the only expense with which you'll have to deal. You'll need to pay commissions, stamp duty, and other closing charges before you're handed the keys to your property. By some estimates, you'll need at least 20,000 pounds in the bank to reasonably invest in a property. Not everyone has this kind of cash lying around.

Rent-to-rent investments remove the need for deposits and mortgages. You aren't putting any cash of your own down other than what you pay the landlord in guaranteed rent. If you know the landlord well enough, you can convince them to accept a monthly arrangement where you pay them every month once you receive rents from your tenants.

This is a great way to get your feet wet in property management and landlording while making money doing so. If you have 5,000 pounds in your bank account, that cash isn't going to be anywhere near enough to finance a BTL or an HMO. However, it will finance a few rent-to-rent properties.

Another advantage is that you'll avoid having to pay all the legal charges that come with buying a property. Since you're renting from the landlord, you don't have to pay stamp charges, property taxes, and all the other charges that come with property ownership. As a result, not only is it cheap to enter a rent-to-rent situation, you'll also close deals quickly, sometimes in a day or two.

Quick Cash Generation

One of the downsides of traditional property investment is that it takes a while for landlords to begin to see returns on their cash investment. This isn't the case with rent-to-rent properties. After all, there's nothing special that you need to do to get the property up and running. Most rent-to-rent situations involve perfectly good properties with uninterested landlords.

All you need to do is come in and start managing the situation properly. You'll earn cash from the first few days if you carry out the process properly. For example, if you source tenants properly, you could earn money from their rental payments within a few days of closing the deal with the landlord.

Note that there are disadvantages, as well. Let's look at some of these now.

Disadvantages

All of the disadvantages of rent-to-rent investing stems from the fact that you don't own the property. The landlord does. As a result, you can find yourself in a worst-of-all-worlds type situation. You need to pay the landlord every month no matter what happens. If you're inexperienced and if the landlord doesn't know you very well, they might insist on multiple months' payment upfront.

Now, you're out of pocket, in charge of maintenance and utility bills and have to find tenants. If tenants leave quickly or don't find the place attractive, you're out of pocket. You don't have property ownership to lean on during tough times. For example, if a landlord doesn't locate tenants for a couple months, and if the rents per month are 800 pounds, they've lost the opportunity to earn (800*2) 1,600 pounds.

However, if property prices increased over that time, they've still made money. As someone who is running a rent-to-rent situation in the same property, you don't have this privilege. You'll lose money if there aren't any tenants. Tenancy voids are a huge risk in rent-to-rent situations and the landlord offloads this risk to you entirely.

There's also a risk of the landlord not holding up their end of the deal. Before entering an agreement, you'll have to discuss how you'll split maintenance expenses. Usually, day-to-day expenses are yours to bear while structural fixes are the landlord's responsibility. For example, if the roof needs repairing, this is usually the landlord's responsibility but if the wiring or plumbing misbehaves, that's your headache.

If the landlord decides to pull out of the deal, you have no recourse. It's their property and they can do as they please with it. You'll have to answer to your tenants if the landlord decides to stop leasing to other people, which is an awkward situation, to say the least.

The key to success with a rent-to-rent is getting to know the landlord well and understanding their motivations. If you aren't comfortable with them for any reason, then don't strike a deal with them no matter how much of a bargain they're offering you. Speak to them extensively and get to know them well. If they've participated in rent-to-rent situations before, ask them how it went and evaluate what went wrong (and right).

If possible, speak to the person they did the rent-to-rent deal with. Watch out for landlords that ask for huge payments upfront and seem concerned only about the money. These people are guaranteed to be unreliable and will cost you money so stay away from them.

RENT-TO-RENT MODELS

There are three ways that you can structure a rent-to-rent situation. Each of these models have their own pros and cons. When looking at them, don't fall into the trap of evaluating their money-making potential. Instead, look for a situation that appeals to you the most. The best deal is one that you can make money from and control well.

Single Let With Discounts

This is the most straightforward deal that you can strike with a landlord. You pay them a discounted amount of rent per month and rent it on the market for the market price. You pocket the difference in the amounts paid. Simple in theory but you'll have to account for maintenance charges and the property's condition.

When running the numbers on the deal, you'll need to make sure that the price differential is enough for you to take care of maintenance and advertising. It's best to have a good marketing plan in place before entering a deal because rental voids will eliminate your profits quickly.

I'll explain how you should analyze rent-to-rent opportunities in more detail shortly. For now, understand that you should carefully look at the property's location and its rental history before committing to a deal.

HMO Conversion

Another popular means of generating rent-to-rent profits is to convert a single to let into an HMO. There are many advantages to this model. Let's say you spot a three bedroom property on the market that was being let to a single family. You can turn this into an HMO and earn more money by letting the bedrooms individually.

If the property has a large living space, you could fashion another bedroom out of it and earn money from that. This boosts your yield and it also removes the need to negotiate aggressively with the landlord. You could theoretically pay market rent to them and still earn a profit.

The downside is that you'll need to get the landlord's approval and you'll need to make sure that your improvements fit the local council's needs. You'll have to register with them as well and bear all costs of maintenance. Landlords might also baulk at converting the property to an HMO since it might violate the terms of their mortgage agreement.

Remember, with an HMO you'll be on the hook for increased expenses since your tenants are greater in number. When done right, converting a single let to an HMO is extremely profitable. You'll need to run the numbers well and make sure you have enough time to manage the property. Remember that you don't have the luxury of outsourcing management and will have to do everything yourself.

A variation of this strategy is to take an underperforming HMO and spruce it up to boost its returns. You'll need to invest more money upfront in these deals so it's likely your ROI will get delayed. For example, if you've invested 5,000 pounds into improvements and are earning 500 pounds as profit every month, it'll be 10 months before you see any cash flow profit from the property.

During those 10 months, you won't have the luxury of leaning on property price appreciation. So make sure that you evaluate the numbers well before choosing to participate in any deal.

Serviced Accommodation

Turning a single let into a serviced accommodation is perhaps the most profitable strategy out there. Serviced accommodation are short-term rentals where tenants stay for a few weeks at most. Due to the short nature of their stay, you can charge a premium. However, you might have to bear improvement costs upfront.

Serviced properties tend to be fully furnished and this increases your initial investment. Aside from the cost of furniture and other appliances, you'll also have to bear the cost of registration with local councils and check whether the landlord's mortgage agreement allows them to operate a serviced accommodation business from their property. In most cases, the lender will not consent to property being used this way.

You'll have to worry about the same kinds of issues as you would with an HMO. Your bills will be greater and your marketing plan needs to be in place to consistently attract people to your property. If you're thinking of Airbnb, then this is one way of marketing your property. The final chapter in this book will cover how you can make money with Airbnb properties.

For now, understand that, despite the promise of greater returns, running serviced accommodation isn't for everyone. You'll have to handle cleaning and maintenance requests by yourself and the transient nature of tenants means that you can't exercise any quality control over them. Also, rental voids are a greater risk here since you'll have high turnover.

This concludes our look at the three rent-to-rent models. As you can see, they have different earning potential, and different pros and cons. When it comes to choosing the right model for you, take your time on hand into account above all else. The potential returns in a deal might be great but it's of no use if you can't make it work. The less money you have, the more time you need to invest.

In rent-to-rent deals, the primary value you're bringing to the table is time. You don't have the money to buy property for yourself so time is all you have. Make sure you use it well and that the profit you're earning from the deal is in line with the amount of time you're investing into it. Don't chase high yields or profits. Always evaluate whether you can make a deal work well for you.

Now, let's look at how you should evaluate rent-to-rent opportunities. There are a few factors to take into account as you can imagine.

ANALYSING RENT-TO-RENT OPPORTUNITIES

Analysing a property for its ability to generate the income you need is critical. With a rent-to-rent opportunity, you need to take the numbers into greater account because your margins will be thin. You'll need to figure out how much to offer the landlord, charge tenants, pay for maintenance, and still have enough leftover every month. Balancing all of these factors is an art as much as it's a science. Here are some of the factors that go into making this decision.

Tenant Demand

Evaluating tenant demand is critical if you want to avoid making a bad deal. Often, landlords will agree to rent-to-rent deals because they can't find anyone who will lease their property. This often happens with HMOs. Some landlords get greedy and convert their single lets into HMOs without taking the location into account.

A property might sometimes work brilliantly as a single let but room sharers might not find the area attractive enough. So always take location into account before moving forward on a deal. It helps to begin in your local area and speak to the real estate professionals present there. Estate agents, landlords, and contactors are good sources of information.

Another way of evaluating tenant demand is to look at property portals. Look at the types of properties present in the area. Are they mostly single lets, HMOs, or some other kind? It's best to stick to the property type that is in the majority in a location. If you see HMOs being advertised the most, then stick with those for your rent-to-rent deals.

Don't get suckered in by a landlord looking to offload their property onto someone who can pay them any amount of cash for it. Do your research and evaluate demand thoroughly. You can figure out rents and other numbers by using the websites I've mentioned thus far in this book (spareroom.co.uk, Rightmove, and Zoopla).

Rents

Technically, rental amounts are attached to demand but rent is important enough to deserve its own section. After all, it's the only form of gain you'll be making on the property. You don't own the property so capital appreciation is not an option. You need to thoroughly evaluate the rental situation in the area before moving on a deal.

Online resources are helpful as is speaking to professionals in the area. A good tactic to employ is to contact a few landlords in those listings and see what you can get in terms of prices. Don't get too aggressive since you might have to approach them down the road for a rent-to-rent! However, this is a good way of gathering market data.

Take note of how long listings last on online channels. If you see a property being advertised for the past six months at a certain price constantly, it means that price isn't acceptable or the property, itself, is poor. Take note of the property's condition, as well. A good property that is well maintained will attract higher rents than a less desirable one.

Often, you'll find properties situated right next to one another demand wildly different rents. The answer lies in their curb appeal and in the way their landlords choose to do business. Renters are very sensitive about these things so make sure you take those conditions into account. Put yourself in a renter's shoes and evaluate properties.

If you're shy about visiting properties yourself, then send a friend or someone you trust and have them take pictures.

This will give you a good idea of what it looks like. It's essential that you visit the location to figure out what the property is like. Also pay attention to who the major employers in the area are. This will give you a rough idea of the kinds of salaries your tenants will earn and how stable it is.

For example, the presence of an insurance company nearby indicates that people who wish to rent are dependent fully on that company. If it hits trouble, then you could be out of luck as well. As I mentioned earlier, look for locations that have a diverse range of employment options at accessible distances.

There are also many websites out there that allow renters to leave reviews of their landlords and properties. Websites such as Asktenants, Marks Out of Tenancy, and Rate Your Landlord are resources you can check. The chances of your property being featured are low but it doesn't hurt to check. If your target renter is a student, then speaking to a few students in nearby campuses is a good move to get their views on rents and locations they'd like to live in.

Net Income and Breakeven Period

Once you've figured out the rental range for the property in question, you can calculate your net income. The net income equation is simple:

Net income = Rent paid to you by tenants - Rent paid to landlord - Maintenance

The tough part of this is figuring out how much you need to set aside for maintenance. Remember that you can negotiate which aspects of maintenance you should take care of with the landlord. Deep structural issues aren't typically your responsibility. If a landlord insists on you covering this, don't be afraid of walking away from a deal.

According to some estimates, it can cost 28% of your rent to maintain your property (Property maintenance costs: How not to blow your budget, 2019). This is an annual figure so the monthly expenses will vary. It's best to categorize maintenance issues into different buckets. You could have exterior maintenance, internal maintenance, structural maintenance, and accessory maintenance. Accessory refers to landscaping and any other parts of the property that improve the tenants' quality of life.

A nicely maintained lawn won't make or break a deal but it allows you to charge more. You could strike a deal with the landlord and have them spruce up certain parts of the property before you take possession. This will allow you to bump rents up and make more money.

Another critical part of figuring out net income is how much you should offer the landlord. If a landlord is used to receiving 1,000 pounds in cash flow from the property, they're unlikely to settle for 500 pounds. There's no template that I can give you to arrive at an ideal price. It depends on the situation. If a landlord has had a property that hasn't been rented for a long time, they're more likely to accept a steep discount.

A landlord who is sick of running around maintaining their property and running it is also more likely to accept a discount. It comes down to figuring out what the landlord's pain points are and giving them a way to solve it through your services. Don't get too greedy with your negotiation. If you find that a landlord is agreeing to everything you say, you're probably offering too much and need to reevaluate your numbers.

Take a look at the property to figure out whether you can boost rents from it. There are many ways of doing this. You could invest your money to make some improvements. For example, changing the door fixtures and taps often gives the property a more luxurious look. These fixtures don't cost much and you can install them yourself. Giving the property a new coat of paint is also a good way to boost rental income potential.

You could offer features that the landlord didn't offer. For example, allowing pets to occupy your property is a huge money spinner. The downside is that you'll have to deal with more damages. It's a risk/reward type situation and you should discuss it with your landlord in detail before moving on it.

The best rent-to-rent opportunities require some work beforehand. A landlord who has a pristine property isn't likely to accept a discount on rent and hand it over to someone else after all. You'll have to invest some money into the property to increase its rental appeal.

A critical part of figuring out the desirability of a deal is to look at how long it will take your net income to pay you your investment back. Remember, you can start calculating returns only once you've made your money back. Many rent-to-rent investors don't understand this basic mathematical fact and rush into poor deals. Let's look at an example to see how the numbers get distorted when you incorrectly calculate your return on investment.

Rent paid to the landlord = 1,000 pounds
Rent received from tenant = 1,500 pounds
Maintenance per month = 300 pounds
Net income = 1500 - 1000 - 300 = 200 pounds
Money invested upfront = 500 pounds

At this point, uninformed investors will calculate their return on investment like this:

ROI = Net income per month/ money invested =
200/500 = 40% per month

As you can see, this is an absurdly high number. Most forms of investment offer 10%–12% per year. Apparently, this property offers 40% per month! However, this is a mathematical trick. The 500 pounds you've invested into the property is gone. If you were to drop the deal once you've invested the money, you can't recover it. Therefore, you need the net income to make that money back first, before you can begin to earn returns on your investment. This is why it makes more sense to calculate a breakeven period, instead of ROI.

Breakeven period in months = Amount invested / Net income earned per month = 500/ 200 = 2.5 months

This means that you'll need to wait for two and a half months before you can begin earning money from the property. If these calculations seem obvious to you, then congratulations, you're unlikely to be swindled by landlords who will push unrealistic numbers onto you. Many first-time investors look at the 40% per month number and rush in without realizing it's a mirage.

Your breakeven period also informs the length of your agreement with the landlord. If your breakeven period lasts a year, then signing a lease for a year makes no sense. You won't make any money. How long should your breakeven period last? This depends on you. Obviously, the smaller it is, the better. However, this isn't always the case with a property.

Generally speaking, you want to avoid getting locked into extremely long-term leases with a landlord. Anything over two years is a bit too long. Once you're in that range, your maintenance problems will increase and many parts of the property will need replacement, instead of mere maintenance. This will increase your costs. Aim to sign leases of up to two years and figure out whether the money you'll make in that time is worth it.

Going back to our previous example, you'll recover your investment in two and a half months, or three months practically speaking, and will make money for 21 months on a two year lease. A net income of 200 pounds per month will give you a total income of (21*200) 4,200 pounds.

Given the amount of time you'll have to spend maintaining the property, is an income of 4,200 pounds over the next two years (roughly 2,100 pounds per year) worth it? Could you do something else and earn more in that period? Let's say that it takes you two hours per day to attend to the property, on average.

What if you could find a part-time job that pays you five pounds an hour, working weekdays only, over the next two years? Your earnings from this job would be:

> Earnings = Money earned per hour * Hours worked per day * number of weekdays per month * number of months = 5 * 2 * 22 * 24 = 5,280 pounds

It looks like the part-time job is the better choice. You'll earn roughly 1,000 pounds more with far less stress with it. Evaluate your options in this manner and see whether the deal numbers make sense for your situation.

Note that the numbers I've used here are not necessarily realistic. There are many people who make rent-to-rent investments work and earn a lot of money from them. So don't get discouraged looking at the miserable numbers I've used in this example.

My point was to highlight that you need to evaluate all of your options. Real estate is a great way to make money, but not every deal is worth entering. So run the numbers and choose your best option.

Terms

You've run the numbers and think the deal is worthwhile to pursue. All that you need to do now is negotiate terms with the landlord. This isn't a simple matter. Most landlords will try to offload significant maintenance costs onto you. Stay away from landlords who don't pursue win-win situations.

What I mean is that some landlords will care just about the money you pay them and won't take your concerns into account. No matter how great the property is, you don't want to ever get into business with such people. Walk away from the deal. You'll always find other opportunities. The best thing to do is to speak to a solicitor who has crafted rent-to-rent agreements previously.

You'll get to understand the nuances of such contracts and what to watch out for. Maintenance is the biggest issue you'll have to negotiate, along with the length of the contract. Remember that the length needs to make sense given your initial investment. For example, let's say you're looking to invest money into sprucing up the property but the landlord insists on a term that won't make you any money. In such situations, you can either negotiate the term length or reduce your upfront investment.

In the latter case, you'll have to evaluate whether the investment still makes sense. Can you earn high rents without the full investment? Will the property still be desirable? Take a look at every aspect of the deal when negotiating.

When negotiating, draw a very clear line with regards to your maintenance responsibilities. This is why you need a solicitor who will specify exact terms in your contract and ensure there aren't any loopholes. Routine maintenance should be your responsibility while deep maintenance involving the structure or major replacements should be the landlord's. Consider imposing a spending limit on maintenance tasks. For example, if any task requires a spend of more than 500 pounds, the landlord has to take care of it.

Maintenance responsibility is why you want to choose landlords that care about their property and your business. A landlord who just wants money isn't going to hold up their end of the deal and you'll have to deal with irate tenants. So discuss all of these matters with a solicitor and craft a bulletproof agreement that protects everyone involved.

SOURCING DEALS

You might be wondering where you can source profitable rent-to-rent deals? Well, there isn't a super secret method to do this. Speak to people in your locality and talk to tradespeople. Get in touch with estate agents and they'll let you know when something comes up. Estate agents can also give you information on the landlord and the state of the property.

Remember that, while the amount of money you make from a single deal might be low, you can always scale your business to earn even more. A single property could bring you 200 pounds but 10 properties will bring you 2,000 pounds per month. So always look to scale your investments when looking at rent-to-rents.

In conclusion, rent-to-rent deals are a great way for you to get into real estate for little to no investment. Make sure you follow the points outlined in this chapter and you'll strike a great deal.

4

BUY-TO-SELL

Buy-to-sell or flipping, as it's commonly known, is an extremely lucrative way of making money from real estate. The premise is simple. You find a property that needs renovation or repairs, repair, and sell it at a higher price. Ideally, the price you can sell it for will be greater than the sum of what you paid to purchase it plus renovation costs.

There are more moving parts to a flip than a simple BTL or HMO investment. For starters, the capital requirements are much higher. Not only do you need to have money to put down as a deposit to purchase the property, you need to have enough cash to repair the place. As a result, you'll usually find experienced investors flipping properties.

However, it's possible for beginners to make money through a flip. The key is to estimate repair costs well and to know when to walk away from a deal. Walking away is much tougher than it sounds. Most flips offer attractive returns and a beginner investor can get caught up in Alice in Wonderland type thinking where they dream of the money they can make without taking costs and risks into consideration.

Let's take a look at some of the most important factors to consider when evaluating a flip.

FACTORS TO CONSIDER

As I said before, there are many moving parts to a flip. You need to align all of them for a deal to successfully go through. On average, you can expect a flip to last between six to seven months. This is a pessimists estimate. Flips that last just three months are possible. If you find your flip extending beyond seven months, then something has gone seriously wrong.

A flip investor makes money when they resell the property after repairs are finished. The longer your property sits on the market, the worse your return is. Speaking of return, you'll find a few property investing literature claiming returns of greater than 100% on flips. There's some inflating going on here. Here's how they arrive at those numbers.

Let's say an investor earns a profit of 10,000 pounds on an investment of 50,000 pounds. Their absolute return is (10000/50000) 20%. Now let's assume they earned this return in two months. On an annualized basis, this return is around 120%. Are you actually earning 120% on your money? Not even close. However, you'll see many investors boost their numbers artificially like this to appeal to people who can give them money to invest.

Don't get carried away by such astronomical numbers. Evaluate every deal, according to the sections that follow.

Location And Other Basics

Location is the most important part of real estate investing. The points I made when talking about BTL properties carry over here as well. You need to understand the basic appeal the property has. For starters, who will want to live in it and why would they find it appealing? What type of property is it? You don't want to renovate an apartment and try to sell it to a family that wants a garden and separate parking space.

The same methods you learned previously with regards to finding prospective buyers and renters applies here, as well. The nature of your exit is important. You could resell it to the market or you could hold onto it. I'll cover exits shortly. For now, understand that you need to tailor your property's location and search to your exit.

Use websites such as Zoopla to look at property trends in your target area. This will let you know what you can expect in terms of sale price as well as how long you can expect your deal to last. Look at how long properties have been on sale in the area. If you notice a large number of properties that have been advertised for sale for the past six months without moving, it's probably a bad time to exit via a sale.

Other location factors to take into account are accessibility and the presence of contractors who can help you rehab the property. If you're looking to refurbish an apartment, what would the neighbors think of the noise and what kinds of restrictions will you have to deal with? There are council codes to abide by as well. Often, you'll find deeply discounted properties on the market that no one wants to touch.

The reason for this is local regulations and the lack of access to the property. Speak to local tradespeople to figure out what you can expect from such a project and the costs associated with a rehab. Of course, it's best to start locally since you'll know the area well. You can use this knowledge to figure out whether a rehab makes sense.

Exit

Your exit strategy is the most important part of a rehab. There are two ways to exit. The first is the quick way, which is to sell the property. The second is the longer way, which is to keep the property and rent it out. In essence, you'll turn the property into a single let or HMO and rent it out.

The way you choose to exit your investment is important because it has repercussions for your financing strategy. You'll learn more about financing shortly. For now, understand that, if you choose to hold onto the property, you'll have to refinance it. The only situation where you won't have to worry about financing is if you have cash on hand. This isn't a realistic possibility so I won't address it.

The first exit, to resell the property, is one that will put cash back into your pocket quickly. Most flippers look to resell as quickly as possible since this gives them cash to invest into their next development. Flippers consider themselves experts at evaluating the property's repair needs. They don't like being landlords and this is why selling is so attractive.

Choosing to hang onto the property is also a good move. Just make sure you're ready to be a landlord or hire a property management firm to run daily operations for you. Having a strategy in place to deal with the less savory aspects of the deal is important when planning an investment. Given the large monetary needs that a flip demands, it's wise to prepare beforehand.

Mind you, you could find yourself having to switch exit strategies as the deal progresses. Right after you finish repairs, you might find that the property market has nosedived and the sale value doesn't justify the expense you've incurred. In such cases, it's best to earn cash flow from the property by leasing it to people. Therefore, it's best to plan for both scenarios beforehand and figure out your plan of action in all of them.

Is one exit better than the other? It comes down to your preferences. The first exit puts cash back into your pocket and you can use this for future investments. This means that you'll earn more money during the course of the year. For example, let's say you earn 20% in three months on your first deal. You then funnel that extra cash into an even bigger deal that earns you another 20% in three months. You then channel that additional cash into two large deals that individually earn you 20%.

Throughout the year, you'll be turning small amounts of cash into even bigger amounts and your overall ROI will be huge. This is how many flippers operate and they can generate in excess of 80% returns, provided their deals workout and they source enough of them. You'll need to have a robust sourcing plan and have good relationships with lenders to arrange financing so that you can move quickly and close on a property.

The second method, which is to hold onto the property and lease it, will boost your net worth significantly. You'll own property at a higher value than what you bought it for, which gives you a significant boost. Furthermore, you can refinance and take your cash out while holding onto the property and collecting rent. I'll explain the cash out refinance method in the next section. It offers the best of both worlds.

Even if you can't pull your cash out, you have a significant capital gain right from the beginning once the property is rehabbed. You can use this increased equity to draw a loan and finance another property purchase such as a BTL or HMO. The key is to have good property management plans in place and to check whether you're willing to be a landlord.

If not, the first exit makes more sense. If the property market heats up significantly and if there's huge demand for your property, you might be better off selling it at inflated prices and waiting to re-enter the market when it cools off.

Financing

Financing is the most important part of the flip. In a flip, you'll be looking at properties that aren't in the best shape. I'm not talking about properties that need a little sprucing up. Most properties will have some kind of structural issue that the current owner cannot fix. The property might be rotting from within for instance. Its roof might need an overhaul and its floors might be falling apart.

Whatever the problem is, you'll need to devote significant resources to fix the place. To do so, you'll need to buy it first. Here's where the problem begins. A bank or traditional lender isn't going to view your purchase favorably. There's too much risk in it for them. Therefore, you're not going to qualify for a traditional or even a BTL mortgage.

More likely than not, you'll receive a loan that falls a little short of a commercial mortgage. These loans are called bridge loans. A flipper uses them to bridge the gap between the purchase and the final sale, hence the name. A bridge loan usually has a higher than normal mortgage rate and will have shorter terms (lengths) than a normal loan. You can expect a bridge loan to last anywhere from a few months to a year. The idea is that you use the loan to fix the property and then find alternate financing solutions to continue holding onto the property.

When looking at a bridge (or bridging) loan you'll notice that interest rates will vary from 0.2% to two percent. Doesn't sound too bad, does it? The thing is, those are monthly interest rates, not annual. You'll pay between 0.2% to two percent per month. That's more than 20% per year and is a significant expense.

While some lenders charge monthly interest, this isn't the only way you can incur this expense. Interest payments could be deferred or rolled up. This means that you'll pay interest at the end of your loan period. Experienced flippers draw bridging loans with term lengths that last just beyond their proposed sale timeline. For example, if they plan on selling the property within six months, they'll draw a loan for seven months or eight.

This way, they can use the excess cash they receive from the sale of the property to pay the bridge lender. As a result, the flipper incurs no interest expense out of pocket. It's a great way to conduct a deal however, you need to be experienced enough to project timelines and account for any unplanned events along the way.

Some lenders will offer you the choice of retained interest. In this model, the flipper borrows the interest as well and pays it back at the end of the loan. You may or may not have to pay interest on this additional borrowed amount (interest on interest). This is a good option if you encounter unforeseen expenses and are confident that the increased sale price will cover these expenses.

You can combine these options with one another as well. You could opt for monthly interest for a few months and then switch to a retained model or vice versa. The better your relationship the lender, the more flexibility you'll have with their terms.

The great thing about bridge loans is that approval is quick and you won't have to worry too much about your poor credit score (if you have one.) Bridge lenders view these loans as risky to begin with so they're not average to lending money to people with poor credit. It's just that they'll add interest onto the loan to cover their risk.

You can expect a decision on your application within 24 hours or less, in most cases. Let's say you decide to hold onto the property once it's been rehabbed. Given the high cost of interest on a bridge loan, it makes no sense to hang onto it. In such situations, the thing to do is to refinance your property via a traditional mortgage.

Since the property is refurbished and has tenants in it (or is in a state to let to tenants), lenders will view it as an acceptable risk. Therefore, you can refinance it with lower interest rates. Here's where you can capture the best of both exits. You've rehabbed the property and, as a result, it's value has increased in the market.

Your bridge loan covers the original value, the amount you paid to purchase it. The excess value that you've accrued is yours entirely. You can now refinance the property for the increased price, have the new lender pay off the bridge lender and pay you cash for the price increase. For example, let's say you bridged a property worth 100,000 pounds and repaired it which caused its value to increase to 150,000 pounds.

Your new lender will offer you financing on the increased property value of 150,000 pounds. As a part of this, they'll pay the old creditor 100,000 pounds and will assume that loan. There's the question of the reamingin 30,000 pounds. Usually, a traditional lender will want you to retain 25% equity in your property. This means that you'll need to retain a value of 37,500 pounds in the new property.

The gain you've experienced on the property is 50,000 pounds. Since you need to retain 37,500, you can borrow the difference in cash from your lender. The lender will pay you 12,500 pounds in cash once the financing deal closes. You can use this cash to invest into the refurbishment of another property. Meanwhile, you continue to own and earn rent from the first property. This rent can cover the mortgage payment on the new, traditional loan.

Thus, you've not only earned a profit on the deal. You've earned steady cash flow through tenants and you've received cash that you can use for your next deal. Note that every lender has different terms when it comes to refinancing. For example, your lender might stipulate that you need to own at least 50,000 pounds in equity in your property. This means, you won't receive a cash payment once you refinance.

If all of this is a bit confusing, then don't worry. You don't have to make cash out refinance work to be successful at flipping properties. Just make sure that the maths with the bridging loan work and plan your exits carefully. If you choose to sell your property, you won't need to worry about refinancing.

Aside from interest, you'll be charged a few other fees as well. These are (Babaee, 2020):

- Arrangement or facility fees - Usually one percent to two percent of the loan amount
- Early exit fee - If you exit the loan early, you'll be charged two percent of the loan amount

- Administration fees - The cost of the paperwork once the loan is finalized
- Legal fees
- Valuation fees- The lender will hire a surveyor to value your property. You'll bear survey costs
- Broker fees - If you use a broker to get in touch with a lender, you'll pay their commission. These fees can amount to as much as six percent of the amount you borrow. Account for them before opting for a loan. If a bridge loan is too onerous for you, you can use other forms of financing. These are:
- Second mortgages - You can draw a second mortgage on your existing property and use that money to finance your flip.
- Remortgage - Refinance your existing mortgage to draw cash out, as explained in the cash out refinance process.
- Secured loan - Post collateral with a lender and borrow money against it
- Personal loan - The borrowed amount will be low but if the bridge loan doesn't cover the entire sale price, you could use this to make up for the deficit

Rehab Costs

Rehabbing the property is the primary task a flipper undertakes. Each flipper has their own area of expertise. For example, you'll find flippers who don't touch properties that have water damage of any kind, while others will seek these out actively. Some love homes that have foundational issues while others will stay away from them.

When you look at a possible flip, it's important for you to understand which niche it falls into. What I mean is, the damage a property has undergone puts it into a niche and attracts flippers who have experience dealing with the issues that the niche presents. Therefore, it's important for you to figure out which niche suits you the best and search for properties that fall within it.

Why is niching so important? In short, it reduces your competition and gives you a great way to differentiate yourself. The truth is that properties that sell at a deep discount requiring minimal rehab are snapped up before they ever touch the market. If you see a flip project on an online portal, it's certain that more experienced investors rejected it. Does this mean those properties are bad bets? Not quite.

They probably have deep issues in areas that the more experienced investors don't specialize in. Also, even if the issues exist in niches that they specialize in, it's probably going to take a lot of work to fix them. After all, if there's easier money elsewhere, why would you spend time on a project that needs a lot of work. This is why the flips that fall into beginner hands require more work.

There are a few red flags to watch out for. Properties that have issues with their foundations are almost always bad bets. It's extremely tough and expensive to fix such a property. Having said that, since no one goes near them, you can niche yourself pretty easily and get access to properties quickly. Make sure that you study the issue well and use reliable tradespeople to fix it for you.

The biggest cause of property damage is water. Whether it's flooding, dampness, leaks, burst pipes, or whatever you can think of, all damage somehow leads back to moisture. When you undertake a project, make sure you strip the home to its bare shell and examine the jousts for rot. It's no use painting the walls a nice color when the shell is rotten. Roof leaks are also common in most rehabs.

Once you've examined the jousts, take a look at the flooring and ceilings. Rot affects them as well so you should have these fixed, if this is the case. Next, inspect the backyard if one exists. If the garden is accessible only through the home, fix the yard before you begin beautifying the property. Call it a lesson I learned the hard way! The last thing you want to do once you've painted and spruced up the place is to cart mud through the home and have to do it all over again.

Next, move onto the wiring and plumbing. Have a professional examine these and reinstall walls and have them painted. Reconfigure the space if you need to, according to your exit strategy, and install new carpets. Give everything a thorough clean and you're all set! Sounds simple doesn't it?

The tricky bit is estimating repair costs and arriving at an offer price. I'll explain how you can do this in the next section. For now, I'd like to focus on the quality of your relationships with tradespeople. They're the ones who will do the work for you so you need to develop a relationship with them before you begin working on your property.

Seek them out and get to know their rates beforehand. They won't be able to give you exact numbers because a lot depends on the extent of the damage, however, get to know the way they work and their methods. When you inspect the property before making an offer, ask them whether they can accompany you. In most cases, they won't since they aren't getting paid to inspect property.

However, take photos and detailed notes of the property so you can show them the damage and get an estimate. Unforeseen expenses will arise if the damage is deeper than in the picture, but you can get within range of the amount of money you'll need to spend by doing this.

Speak to the property owner as well and ask them about the damage the property has sustained. Most people will frankly tell you what's wrong with the place. Don't expect them to go into great detail since this reduces their leverage, but in some cases where the seller is desperate, they might be an open book. Look for clues as to how well the property was maintained before you arrived, the type of people who lived there and so on.

There are some standard expenses you'll have to undertake once you land a flip. You'll have to replace the carpet, cabinets, electrical fixtures, and taps/faucets. In some cases, the flooring will also have to be replaced. The good news is that, aside from flooring, everything else is quite cheap. Local rates vary so make sure you check with tradespeople what they cost.

Another good way of figuring out costs is to visit an appliance store or a home improvement outlet. These stores usually have salespeople who were formerly in the trades. They'll give you practical advice and help you to figure out costs. The retail prices at these outlets will be higher than what you'll pay in your project. However, those prices give you a good baseline to estimate costs.

Making an Offer

Your offer price is the most important part of the deal. It's a summation of everything you've done so far to estimate the value of the property and your profit. So how should you go about making an offer and determining the right price? Let's examine the profit equation for a flip first:

Profit = Sale price of rehabbed property - Rehab costs - Purchase price

You can estimate the sale price by looking at comparable properties in the area. This is your ceiling. You need to make sure that you have enough room between this number and your purchase price to account for your profit, rehab costs, and any unforeseen expenses. Usually, it's best to estimate an error margin of 10% with rehab costs. This means that, if you budget 5,000 pounds for rehab, account for it as being 5,500 pounds.

However, you might incur greater costs. Therefore, the best way to arrive at a purchase price is to use the 70% rule I mentioned previously. If you've forgotten, here it is:

Offer/purchase price <= 70% of (Sale price of rehabbed property - Rehab costs)

For example:

> Sale price of rehabbed property = 150,000 pounds
> Rehab costs (with 10% margin or error) = 5,500 pounds
> Offer/purchase price should be <= 0.7*(150000-5500) = 101,150 pounds

Obviously, the lower the number, the greater your profit is. This offer price is a 33% discount from prevailing market prices. The seller will be thinking in these terms so it's important for you to frame your offer in terms of the costs you'll incur. As a rule of thumb, the greater the price of the property is, the more you'll need to spend rehabbing it. As a beginner, it's best to stick to lower priced properties.

If you're unable to find enough wiggle room in between the rehabbed value and the offer price, then consider changing the property's configuration. You could add some features to it to boost its value. Investments, such as high end appliances, an additional bedroom, better toilets, etc. add considerable value. If the property has a garden, for example, you could extend the living space into the garden and reduce its footprint.

Obviously, you'll need to take quality of life into consideration. This is why it's important to thoroughly understand the location and the kind of people it attracts.

However, the 70% rule almost always helps you arrive at a sensible offer price.

Taxes And Legalities

Many property investors fail to take the effect of taxes into account when designing investment strategies. Flippers have to be especially aware of the way taxes work since it can affect your choice of exit. First off, you might have to pay capital gains taxes. Many property flippers try to use loopholes to avoid taxes. Needless to say, these loopholes don't offer much benefits.

One of the more famous loopholes is the tax break that allowed people to sell a second home without incurring high capital gains taxes. You'll hear many flippers talk of this rule but this isn't the case anymore. Previously, the rule allowed owners of second homes to avoid paying taxes on the sale for up to 36 months. The idea was to give homeowners a break if they struggled to sell their homes in tough markets.

The government has now reduced the exemption period from 36 to 18 months. So don't think you can avoid paying taxes for three years after selling your property. The kind of tax you pay is the next thing to consider.

You could end up paying trade taxes or capital gains taxes. Contrary to popular perception, you won't automatically pay capital gains taxes. Trade taxes are 45% plus national insurance while capital gains taxes are at 28%. On the surface of it, trade taxes seem like a bad deal. However, the matter is more nuanced than that.

For starters, you'll need to determine whether you're engaged in a trade or not. If your intention when buying the property was to fix it and flip it, you're engaged in trade. However, intention is a mental choice and no one can positively prove this. Therefore, a few flippers look to take advantage of this loophole by delaying the sale of the property. For example, if you sell the property back into the market within three months of purchasing it, it's pretty easy to decipher that your intent was to trade it.

However, what if you hold it for six months? A year? In such cases, intent is tougher to prove. This is a loophole that you can exploit but don't overdo it. Courts and HMRC look at your pattern as well. If they notice a string of properties that you've held onto for a few months and then sold, this will be used as evidence of trade tax evasion which is a far harsher penalty than the higher trade tax rate (Flipping property, 2018).

Besides, the trade tax isn't as bad as it seems. While the rate is higher than the capital gains rate, you can claim rehab expenses as deductions. Therefore, you're only taxed on the profits of your trade. With capital gains taxes, the amount taxed is the entire monetary gain, ignoring rehab costs. For example, let's say you rehab a property by investing 20,000 pounds into it and realize a gain of 50,000 pounds upon selling it.

Your true profit on this deal is (50000-20000) 30,000 pounds. Trade taxation will have you paying 45% of this amount which comes to 13,500 pounds. Capital gains taxes are at 28% but you can't claim expenses. Therefore, you'll pay 28% of 50,000 which is 14,000 pounds.

The implication here is that, if your rehab costs are high, it's better to sell the property and eat the trade tax. If your costs are low, then hang onto the property and rent it out. You'll earn cash flow on it and recover your rehab costs, plus claim the mortgage interest tax credit and deduct maintenance expenses over time. When you sell it, you'll pay capital gains taxes on the price increase, having used cash flow to recover your rehab expenses.

Note that if you're operating under a development company or a private limited, you'll incur trade taxes no matter what.

As you can see, there are many considerations that go into making a flip successful. Take your time and make sure you've worked out the maths before jumping into a deal. Much like with the other investment strategies, the best places to source a flip are online, estate agents, tradespeople, and other real estate professionals. The financial investment is greater in a flip but the rewards are greater as well.

5

PROPERTY DEVELOPMENT

Property development combines all of the strategies you've learned thus far into a single, profitable business opportunity. When developing property, your primary aim is to generate a profit irrespective of the strategy you use. You could buy property cheaply and refurbish it into an HMO. You could flip it back into the market. You could improve it a little bit and sell it for a small profit. Or you could buy land and build properties from scratch. The choice is entirely up to you.

What makes property development different from the other strategies discussed is that you'll almost always have to incorporate yourself through a PLC or some legal structure. By doing this, you'll build more credibility for yourself in the market and can proudly call yourself a property developer. However, this step isn't always necessary. If you have access to financing, you can carry out your business in your name.

The reason investors choose to incorporate is that it makes raising money easier. If you wish to access private investor funds, you can sell shares in your company to them and raise money. New companies notoriously find it difficult to gain access to finance property purchases. Private investor funds offer a great way to jump over this hurdle.

Once you have a successful track record of development, you'll find banks lining up to offer you financing. The strategies you'll follow are the same as the ones you've already learned. You'll have to tailor your strategy to the property's situation. For this reason, experienced investors choose to go down the property development route.

The only difference is you'll have access to a greater number of sources to find deals. Let's look at some of them.

HOW TO SOURCE DEALS

Driving your car around a neighborhood and speaking to the locals is the tried and true method of unearthing the best property deals. However, as a developer you can use a few more professional sources. Keep in mind that the average deal size will be greater than what an individual investor might look at.

This is why you'll find people ready to bring deals to you. For example, an estate agent might focus on sourcing single lets for an individual investor. If they know a property developer is looking for deals, they'll expand their search and bring deals that are worth millions of pounds. It comes down to how strong your balance sheet is and the size of your funds.

For this reason, it's best to go down the property development route once you have access to a large amount of funds and can reasonably take on at least three or four properties at once. Anything below that and you're better off going down the individual investor route already described in previous chapters.

Estate Agents, Online Listings, And Tradespeople

These three sources of property deals are ever-present. It's just that you'll have a larger bankroll to play with and you'll find these sources more helpful to you. You can specify exactly what you're looking for and turn these sources loose. Online portals contain a ton of listings but remember that the deals you find there have already been rejected by another experienced investor.

This isn't a bad thing, as I explained in the previous chapter, but you need to evaluate whether the deal is a good fit for you. Don't rush into a property just because it's advertised as high yield or a great opportunity. Location plays an important role as always so be patient and great deals will come to you.

A good way to use estate agents is to turn them loose and have them find you deals that aren't on the market, or that aren't even on the existing property owner's mind. Given the property shortage that the UK is experiencing, this method of sourcing deals is gaining traction. It's called infilling and your relationship with estate agents is the key to success.

An infill is a piece of property that hasn't been fully developed. For example, when a neighborhood gentrifies, older properties such as grocery stores, launderettes, and other small businesses will continue to operate from their old locations as the neighborhood improves. You can buy these properties and develop them for a profit.

You'll pay a sizable price for these properties since their value will have risen. However, infills are all about value addition. Once you improve the property or change its character, you'll earn a windfall. This will take you into the realm of commercial property development as well, but banks are more than willing to underwrite such loans. This is because the surrounding neighborhood has risen in value and the project carries less risk than a brand new development.

Local councils favor these projects since it enhances property values in the area. Any disused roads or abandoned office parks are great opportunities for you to step in and add value. Just be careful to think everything through at first and don't be in a rush to close the deal. Infills are an expensive proposition and require a lot of coordination to make a success of.

Auctions

Property auctions are a great way to snap up deals but things can get out of hand if you aren't careful. Auctions occur when the existing owner of the property cannot make payments. Banks seize the property and auction it off to recover costs. Often, these properties sell for far less than their market value.

You might be wondering why I haven't included auctions as a source of deals for individual investors thus far? This is because the auction environment can create problems for inexperienced investors. An auction is designed to deliver the highest prices for all properties involved. The auction house is only interested in stirring up a bidding frenzy.

As a result, an inexperienced investor risks losing their head and overbidding. This is why you'll find a large number of experienced investors at property auctions. They aren't for the timid or inexperienced. You'll have to quickly figure out whether the bid price is worth it for you and you'll have to take the rest of the escrow into account.

Bidding prices often start extremely low but if the property is a hot one, prices can rise dramatically. The best way to find auction listings is to approach banks and inquire about any auctions they have scheduled. These days, most banks publish auction listings on their website.

If you have access to enough cash, you can approach banks and offer to buy properties in bulk from them. I'll cover this in a later chapter but this is a great way to gain control over a large number of properties before they hit the auction block.

Site Finding Agents

Also called property sourcers, these agents serve property developers and usually focus on bulk deals. Bulk here refers to more than one property in a package. Typically, they charge fees equal to two percent of the deal size. Needless to say, they prioritize big investors since they can earn more fees.

However, smaller property sourcers often have single lets and single HMOs on their portfolio since they're too small for a large developer to make money off. These smaller sourcers are your best bet when starting out. The best way to get in touch with them is to speak to an estate agent and have them put you in touch with people. If you spread the word about looking to get into property development, odds are that one of these agents will get in touch with you.

Site finding agents will also give you complete information on a property's history and the potential ways in which you can add value to it. You'll pay for this service, of course, but it's worth it if you can source a steady stream of opportunities. Be selective and don't be pressured into entering a deal you aren't sure about.

Professional Referrals

If you're entering property development, odds are that you've been around for a while and have a decent-sized network in the industry. You'll know solicitors, agents, tradespeople, and interior designers. These people are invaluable sources of information so keep expanding your network. Eventually, one of these people will let you know of a potential deal.

FINANCING

As with every real estate project, figuring out financing goes a long way towards ensuring your success. With property development, there are many ways of securing financing. This is because of the variety of strategies you can use. You'll even have access to commercial finance and this is a completely different world with its own considerations.

The traditional sources and types of financing still apply to property development. For example, you can opt for BTL mortgages or mortgages on HMO property. Remortgaging your existing property or relying on your cash savings are perfectly valid ways of raising funds. You can also apply for a cash advance with your existing lender to fund a property development.

We've already covered the basics of how these options work so I'm not going to spend time going over them again. The process isn't different if you're a property developer. You'll need to justify the maths behind the deal to a lender and they'll offer you an interest rate based on how risky they think the project is.

When you dabble in property development, you'll have the option of developing commercial property. For example, you could refurbish commercial shops on a high street. You can't use traditional mortgages that apply to residential property to develop these. You'll need a commercial mortgage.

Commercial Mortgages

The commercial mortgage process is more strenuous than its residential counterpart. For starters, your deal's numbers are extremely important. The lender will pay close attention to them and will also evaluate your expertise with regards to ensuring the success of the deal. This is why commercial property development isn't suitable for beginners. They're unlikely to find financing.

If you find a good commercial deal but can't arrange the financing, consider passing it onto another developer and either buying equity in the deal or charging a finder's fee. I'll discuss these methods shortly. For now, keep in mind that the commercial mortgage process takes longer than a residential one.

The lender will send an appraiser to evaluate the property and this will determine how much they'll lend you. More often than not, the appraiser's valuation will differ from the commercial potential of the property. It isn't out of the ordinary for commercial developers to seek bridge financing to help them tide over short-term cash flow problems caused by such appraisals.

The other thing to keep in mind is that you will need a solicitor's assistance throughout the process. Commercial deals need to be foolproof and for this reason, it's best to use the services of an experienced solicitor throughout the process. You'll hear some investors scoff at this notion but it's better to pay for legal services and protect yourself than it is to risk property forfeiture because your lease terms weren't secure enough.

You also want solid legal backing because commercial landlording is a different kettle of fish from residential landlording. As a commercial landlord, you're exposed to greater liability claims and you'll need stronger insurance. For example, if your tenant's customer falls and injures themselves on your property, you might be liable for damages even if you have nothing to do with the tenant and their business.

The structure of your lease will also play a role in determining liability. Many commercial landlords take a cut of their tenants' revenues and charge them a minimum rent per month. When it comes to liability claims, this structure might implicate you as a stakeholder of the business unit's location and you could be found liable. There are also building codes and safety regulations you need to adhere to.

All of these factors play a role in financing. The mortgage that underwrites an office block is very different from one that backs a retail outlet on a high street. To make sense of everything you need the services of a solicitor and tradespeople that understand codes and will keep you compliant.

BUILDING A TEAM

As a developer, one of the most important tasks you can undertake is assembling a team that can help you bring your vision to life. There are two ways to go about doing this. The first is to hire a company or a consultancy that will take care of everything for you. The second is to do everything yourself by hiring your team. The second option makes sense if you have the capital and a large number of developments. You'll also need a steady stream of property opportunities to keep your team busy.

Most beginner developers choose the first option since it's easy, even if it cuts into the margins. However, this is a good trade because of the sheer number of tasks you need to take care of. Before going into the steps you'll have to execute, let's quickly look at who you need to have on your team.

Your Team

At the very least, your team needs to have a property accountant. Not only will this person keep you compliant and file your accounts on time, they'll also save you money through tax credits and relief from the government. If you hire an accountant full-time, you can use their skills to run the numbers on a prospective project to check whether it makes sense for you. Don't fret about the cost of hiring an accountant. Their fees are fully tax deductible.

You'll also need a property lawyer or a firm that can walk you through the minefield that is property law in the UK. Each council has different building codes and you'll also have to take national laws into account, especially the environmental ones these days. A lawyer will keep you on the right side of the law so invest in one.

Some property developers choose to go after financing by themselves but this is an inefficient way of going about it. It's far better to work with a finance broker who can give you access to their special relationships in the industry. If broker fees impact your margin adversely, then you're probably not in the right deal to begin with.

Construction and commercial finance mortgages are complex and there are many ways of structuring a deal. A broker will help you find the best solution so invest in a good one. On the operations side of things, you'll need to hire an architect or draughtsman who understands local council codes. They'll immediately let you know whether your strategy with a property is feasible or not. For example, you might set out trying to convert a bunch of single lets into HMOs but the local council might object to too many partitions being erected.

Someone who closely works with the architect is a surveyor. These people survey the land and run subdivision studies on it. They'll have the best local knowledge. They're not to be confused with a quantity surveyor. These people help you to apply for and receive tax rebates upon project completion. Many developers leave money on the table by not maximizing these rebates so don't make that mistake.

Lastly, you need a builder to physically erect your plans. You want to choose builders that are experienced and large enough to offer you prices lower than retail on building materials and so on. A large builder will bring economies of scale to the table and you can take advantage of this. Often, builders have readymade plans of villas and apartments that you can use, thereby saving you the cost of hiring an architect. It's still a good idea to hire a local architect to validate council codes.

There are many moving parts to a development project and everything needs to be coordinated properly. When you're starting out, it's best to hire a project manager or management firm that can coordinate all of the activities you need to carry out. You'll find many project management firms offering all of the other services within a package.

It's best to hire your own professionals and tradespeople since you'll save money by doing this.

Stages of Development

There are different stages to a property development project. Note that you won't have to execute all of them since a lot depends on the type of project you're undertaking. Once you've located a property and arranged financing tentatively (based on rough numbers and applying for pre-approval with the lender), you need to conduct a feasibility study.

To do this, you first need to use a solicitor's services to scan the purchase contract for any anomalies. You'll also need to hire an architect and a surveyor to help you figure out local council guidelines and the practicality of your strategy. This is where you'll figure out how many units your property will finally have, what kinds of refurbishment you'll carry out, and any remodeling needs.

Take special note of any trees on your site since they can't be cleared at will. You'll have to refer to the council's environmental guidelines before you can decide what to do with them. It's often best to build around them since it improves the quality of life of the people who will ultimately live in the property.

Your architect will develop final plans in accordance with council requirements. At this stage, you can take them to a builder and figure out costs. Choosing a builder is an important step and it's best to spend some time evaluating them before your project begins. Different builders specialize in different types of projects. Some specialize in commercial property while others specialize in single lets exclusively.

The location you've chosen also determines the kind of builder you'll hire. A builder that specializes in luxury property is hardly a good fit for a project in a lower socio-economic area. Their financial standing is important as well. If the builder is in a poor state and goes into administration when your project is underway, you'll face delays and project cost overruns. Ask them for financial statements and credit reports. Don't work with someone that is close to the brink. Check their existing projects for build quality and make sure it's up to the standard you're looking for. A builder that is confident of their delivery quality will offer to show you around past projects unprompted.

When crafting a contract with a builder, have your solicitor craft an agreement. Make sure you include clauses that protect you in case of delivery delays and other problems. Time extensions are routine in the business and you need to negotiate clauses that make sense for you. Clearly define processes and extension procedures. It's best to set an expense cap on these extensions to ensure that you don't have a project that has runaway costs.

Lastly, check with their previous clients for references and reviews. It's also a good idea to speak to subcontractors to get an idea of how the builder handles their business. Often, poor quality builders will present a friendly face to you since you're the client but will execute less than ethical business practices with their subcontractors. Speak to them to get a true understanding of who you're dealing with.

At this stage, you should also introduce yourself to the planning department of the local council to make sure there aren't any regulatory surprises in the offing. Future zoning considerations and other proposed changes can delay your project. A good surveyor and architect will be aware of any possible objections and will alert you in advance.

Make sure that your architect's designs are geared for fastest approval. Remember, you haven't taken possession of the property as yet. If your application is stuck in council review, another developer could swoop in and take control of the property. Speed is essential when designing your plans and submitting them for approval.

Once your plans are approved, it's time to arrange financing and negotiate a sale price. Follow the tips I'll talk about in the final chapter in this book to ensure a mutually beneficial negotiation. Once you purchase the property, you'll submit the final plans to the council. They might require further changes so this step takes a while. Your architect and surveyor will be the people who will help you to figure out what needs to be done.

Your architect will prepare detailed drawings and many councils require these to be signed off by an engineer. Depending on the complexity of the project you will need the approval of geotechnical, structural, and civil engineers. Councils have a list of firms that you'll need to approach for approval. If you have an engineer on your payroll, you can present them as a qualified candidate as well. However, third party oversight over the approval process will be necessary.

Once all plans are in place, it's time to begin construction. Often, architects will supervise the construction and ensure everything is being built to spec. At this stage, a quantity surveyor also plays an important role. They're the ones who will make sure that your project doesn't go over budget. If you've sought financing greater than a million pounds, your lender will insist on appointing a quantity surveyor.

As the builder hits their milestones, you'll need to release payment to them. Typically, these milestones are agreed upon ahead of time and your quantity surveyor will ensure all payment terms and deliverables are on spec. At every stage of completion, your architect and surveyor will have to ensure that the project has been executed according to regulations and council codes.

Once the project is complete, you'll have to carry out subdivision and obtain separate titles for each living unit, depending on the situation. If you've built a single HMO, then separate titles aren't necessary. An apartment block will need separate titles. You now have a chance to execute one of your exit strategies.

Exit Strategies

There are two ways you can exit your property investment. The first is to sell the property on to someone else and earn a profit. The second is to hang onto it and earn rents. Let's look at the first method. There are two ways you can execute this step. Most builders will incorporate their exit strategy as a means of raising money.

The way they do this is by marketing their property as an investment while it's in the construction stage. This is called off-plan property marketing and I'll discuss this in more detail in a following chapter. However, as a developer, you could market your property and attract buyers for individual units. You'll charge them at the same milestones as would your builder and therefore earn a profit at every step.

The flip side is that you'll have to incur marketing costs. In competitive markets, it can be tough to stand out and this will drive your costs higher. Another option is to sell the fully developed property. However, this places a cash flow burden on you during the development phase. Most developers look to strike a balance between these two options.

The second exit strategy is to hold onto the property and earn rent from it. It boosts your asset values and allows you to borrow against it in the future to fund more developments. Most developers hold onto their first property development so as to place it as collateral for future mortgages. This allows them to scale their business rapidly.

The issues you'll face with this approach is that you'll have to rely on debt to fund your first two projects at the very least. You won't recover your investment as a cash profit since you won't be selling your property. This means that, if the market goes against you in the short-term, you'll have a truckload of debt to payoff and a poor market to sell into. This can put considerable strain on finances as you can imagine.

Evaluate the pros and cons of both exit strategies carefully and use your accountant's inputs before deciding on an approach. It's important for you to consider timelines when choosing an exit. A project usually takes anywhere from six months to two years to complete. The longer the project is, the more an incremental exit by selling off-plan properties makes sense. For shorter timelines, you can hold onto the property and earn rental income to improve your cash flow.

In conclusion, property development is a profitable business but you need to carefully consider all of the costs and issues that might occur. It's best suited for investors who already have experience handling properties and are well versed with the markets into which they're looking to enter. Take your time evaluating the numbers behind a deal and don't be in a rush to cash in your profits.

6

BUYING OFF-PLAN

You might have heard of off-plan properties previously and might have shied away from them. It's true that buying off-plan properties aren't for the faint of heart. It can be tough to pay money for something that doesn't even exist as yet, with the developer's word as the only guarantee that you'll have a tangible asset at the end of it all.

However, there are many advantages to buying off-plan. I'll cover some of them later in this chapter. For now, let's look at what off-plan properties are and how you can go about buying them,

WHAT ARE THEY?

An off-plan property is something that hasn't been built as yet. In some cases, the foundation might not have been laid as yet. Many home buyers are discouraged by this and you'll find mostly property investors and speculators operating in off-plan properties. The key to ensuring off-plan success is to evaluate your exit strategy.

Speculation is quite common in off-plan properties since you won't have to invest too much in the development, other than the deposit, and you can resell or assign the property to someone else at a later date to capture a good profit. There is almost guaranteed appreciation with off-plan properties since the value addition is obvious.

The first purchaser of an off-plan property is buying a hope and dream essentially. As the final building takes shape, the property's value increases significantly, sometimes by as much as 15%–30%. The flip side is that the property might never get erected. There is a simple step-by-step process you can execute when it comes to buying off-plan properties.

Source Good Properties

The first step is to source the right property. You shouldn't pick any old thing when it comes to buying off-plan properties. There are a few considerations you must take into account before investing your money. The most obvious is the developer's reputation. Look for a steady string of development success before investing in a property. Often, beginner or under-capitalized developers sell off-plan properties in an attempt to reduce their financing burden.

If you know the developer well and are confident of the plan's success, then it's worth investing. However, it's generally better to invest with developers that have a track record of success. Another aspect to take into account is their plans for the property and the location. When scouting the location, use the same process as previously described in this book. Make sure it holds appeal to prospective buyers and renters.

The developer's plan for the property also needs to make sense. Since everything is off-plan, it might be tough to envision the final development. A red flag to watch out for is the developer trying to build as much as possible within the land they've purchased. All you'll end up with is a concrete jungle that has no appeal to the people who might actually want to live in that location.

Be prepared for plans to change. Often, due to financing constraints, developers will rework plans to save money or might even scrap a portion of the development. The likelihood of this happening with larger developers is smaller but it's not impossible. Larger developers might finish their off-plan properties' construction in phases. For example, they'll finish one block of towers before completing another and so on.

If you're looking to resell the first property, then keep in mind your buyer might have to live in a quasi-construction site for a few months or years until the entire area is fully developed. Your exit also determines what sort of property you should be looking at. If there's potential for a deal, you can enter something that looks a bit risky on the surface. However, if the market is about to go bad or if no one is willing to buy the property off you, then you might have to carry the property and eventually rent it in an attempt to recover your investment.

Financing

Financing is a bit tricky with off-plan properties. For starters, your property doesn't exist. This means banks and lenders won't underwrite conventional mortgages for you. You'll receive an initial mortgage that covers the property until it's fully developed. You might even have to reapply for financing one the property is complete, assuming you haven't resold the property as yet.

Financing also hinges on how far off-plan your property is. If it's 18 months down the road, then you won't need a mortgage until it's six months out and will have to pay a deposit of around 20%–25% as the project nears completion.

The mortgage application process for an off-property isn't all that different from the process for a finished property. If you're looking to reassign the property before it's complete or in completion, it's best to work with a mortgage broker who understands the process well and can connect you with the right lenders.

Often, conventional lenders will hesitate to underwrite an off-plan purchase. This is where a mortgage broker with off-plan experience will help you immensely. Once you have financing in place, you'll need to pay the developer a reservation fee. This is usually around 1,000 pounds.

Legalities

Once you pay your reservation fee, the legal process begins. You'll have to appoint a conveyancer to handle the legalities of your purchase. A conveyancer is just a property solicitor who specializes in drafting legal contracts for property purchase. Once they draft a contract, you'll exchange paperwork with the lender and the developer, and can take possession of the property.

Of course, there is no property for you to take hold of as yet. You'll pay the deposit based on agreed upon milestones throughout the course of completion.

Wait

This step is the most nerve-wracking one. Once the deposit is paid, all you can do is wait for everything to be completed. If the developer you've chosen is a reputable one, you won't have much to worry about. There is the possibility that things might be delayed. As the property is being developed, you'll have the opportunity to specify design characteristics, such as layout options and other aesthetic choices.

When specifying these, make sure you don't customize it too much. You'll either be selling the property or hanging onto it with an aim of earning rental income from it over time. Ideally, your property will hold appeal to as many people as possible so make it homely but don't overdo it.

Before completion, you should run a snagging survey to make sure everything is in order. Snagging surveys are intended to unearth problems with a property before it's fully completed. Often, developers won't allow such surveys to be completed. It's best to prepare ahead of time and use your solicitor to prepare legal justification for access to the property before completion.

If you find issues, alert the developer immediately and, depending on their response, you might have to initiate legal action. Make sure you document all communication and lean on your solicitor (conveyancer) to ensure your rights are upheld.

Exit

Once the property is complete, it's time to execute your exit. You can either flip the property for a profit or you can hang onto it and earn rent from it. Flipping the property is speculative but, in a hot property market, it might be the best move to make. Just be prepared to hold onto the property in case something unexpected happens.

If you're going to hold onto the property, you will need to rearrange financing. This is as simple as reapplying with your lender. You'll typically receive better financing terms and rates once you do this since the property is complete.

PROS AND CONS AND OFF-PLAN PROPERTIES

As you can see, there are a few risks involved with buying off-plan properties. However, these are balanced out by the rewards on offer. Let's look at some of the advantages of buying off-plan.

Advantages of Buying Off-Plan

The biggest advantage of buying off-plan properties is the property appreciation. An off-plan property will always sell for less than market rate and, depending on how long it takes to fully build the property, you could end up earning a huge profit. For example, if you buy the property at a 20% discount and if the developer completes building it within six months, you've earned almost 40% on an annualized basis (20*2).

If the development is a brand new one and if the location is being revamped as part of a broader plan, you'll realize even greater gains. If you encounter a hot property market, gains of 20% aren't unrealistic. Of course, you shouldn't invest in a property solely on the basis of the gains on offer. You should take every other factor into account as well.

Another advantage of buying property off-plan is the ability to customize it. You can change the floor plan to suit your exit strategy. Most developers will allow you to customize the property up to a certain extent so don't think you can redesign the entire place.

Developers will also offer you the ability to exit the contract before completion. This is called reassignment. Most developers will allow you one reassignment before completion. This means if property prices in an area have increased massively since you purchased the place, you can reassign or sell it to someone else to capture that profit.

Reassignment is carried out by using your lawyer's services. The developer will also be involved in the process (Reassignments—what actually are they?, 2020). Once reassignment is complete, you'll be able to transfer the property, receive your deposit back, and the profit you've earned.

Another advantage of buying off-plan is that the new property will be covered by NHBC (National House Building

Council) for up to 10 years. Note that this warranty covers the exterior of the building. You're also covered for up to 10% of your deposit should the builder go bust or out of business before the property is complete.

Disadvantages

The biggest risk with off-plan properties is that the developer might not hold up their end of the deal. Project delays and other developer failures can jeopardize your property investment. Your money will be stuck in the project and there's nothing you will be able to do to extricate it. Often, beginner or first-time developers overreach and discover they're grossly under-capitalized. This is why it's best to stick to experienced operators who have a successful track record.

Securing financing for an off-plan property is tricky if you try to arrange it by yourself. The services of a mortgage broker might cost you money but you'll save more in the long run. The vagaries of the property market are also a risk. If your aim was to flip the property into a good market, you might find that the nature of the market has changed and you'll have to hold onto your property longer than imagined.

Therefore, always have a backup plan in place and be realistic about how much you can borrow. It's better to cover your risks before looking at potential rewards when it comes to off-plan property investment.

7

AIRBNB

If you live in an area that is appealing to tourists, you've definitely heard of Airbnb by now. In fact, you might have noticed some of your neighbors placing rooms in their properties on Airbnb for rent. So how profitable is this and is it worth your time? There are two ways of monetizing Airbnb.

The first is to rent out rooms in your property to tourists and short-term renters. The second is to conduct a rent-to-rent strategy using Airbnb. The second model is practiced more often. Airbnb is a supercharged version of regular buy-to-let and rent-to-rent strategies since your turnover will be much higher. You'll also need to figure out how you can make your property stand out on the website. With more properties being listed everyday, this is a tougher task than you might first think.

The flip side is that Airbnb can bring you a far greater amount of profit than a conventional strategy. Most Airbnb renters stay for short periods of time and this means you can charge higher prices and earn more money over a month than a regular landlord. Let's look at some of the best ways of making money through Airbnb listings.

HOW TO USE AIRBNB

The primary key to Airbnb success is actually out of your control. It has to do with a location's touristic appeal. If you're living in Shrewsbury or Norwich, there aren't going to be too many tourists flocking to visit your property, no matter how much you love your hometown. If your place isn't touristy, then it's best to drop Airbnb as a means of making money. More conventional methods will suit you.

If your property is in a place that tourists love to visit, then you need to get to work enhancing your property's appeal. Remember that you don't have to own property to advertise it on Airbnb. You can use a rent-to-rent strategy on it instead. You can lease the property from the landlord for, say 1,500 pounds per month, and advertise it on Airbnb for 2,000 pounds per month.

The trick is to make sure your listing shows up as high as possible on the listings. So how do you do this? Here are a few tips that will ensure your property gets clicked on routinely.

Service Fees

Airbnb breaks down rental costs by listing the rental price and the service fees separately. In some locations, you'll see this displayed as a cleaning fee. You can use this fee to collect the same amount of money but display your property as being a good bargain. For example, let's say that most properties in your location are listed as having a rent of 70 pounds per night.

You could advertise your property at a rate of 60 pounds per night and charge the additional 10 pounds as a cleaning/service fee. The listing page only highlights the nightly rate, not the cleaning fee. Once a customer clicks onto your listing page, they'll be able to view the full cost.

Conversion rates on clicks are pretty high with Airbnb so if a customer likes your photos (next tip) and likes the reviews, they're more likely than not going to reserve your property. Don't go overboard with service fees though. You shouldn't list a rent of one pound per night and service fees of 69 pounds. That's ridiculous and Airbnb will boot you off their platform if you do this.

Photos

Your property's photos and headline are the most important parts of your listing. Invest in good photos. Unless you're a photographer yourself, don't think that an iPhone will do the job. You should hire a professional photographer to take photos of your place. You want to take as many photos as possible but don't overdo it.

For example, most listings have a sweet spot of 15–16 photos. Listings that have 40–50 photos are overdoing it, no matter how huge your property is. If your place has a few quirks, don't shy away from them. Highlight them in your photos. If your place has a sloped roof that limits space in one of the bedrooms, highlight photos that display this.

Your objective should be to give your prospective guests as much information as possible. If you can't make the property appealing without resorting to trickery, then the property is the wrong one.

Enhance Appeal

Airbnb gives you many ways of enhancing your property listing's appeal. The most obvious one is the headline. This is the text that a user views in the search results list. Keep it simple and to the point. Don't stuff it with all caps LIKE THIS or use words such as HOT DEAL or variations of this. If your property is a good find, Airbnb highlights this automatically.

Instead, highlight its location and space to get people clicking onto your detailed listing. Describe your property in great detail in the listing page. Note all tourist attractions and holiday activities that people like doing. If your property has any notable features, such as a workspace or a kitchen, note this as well and make sure you take good photos to highlight these features.

At the very least, your detailed property description should be at least three paragraphs long. Be flexible with your check in and check out times. List fixed times on your listing page but if a person contacts you about checking out later or earlier, accommodate them as long as it doesn't inconvenience anyone else. Remember that people are typically on vacation so make it as stress-free as possible for them.

It's a good idea to partner with local tourist companies or even create your own little touristic activity to enhance appeal. Partnering with a tourist company allows you to highlight this fact in your description and you can position yourself as a one stop solution for everything your tenant needs.

Creating your own activity allows you to take advantage of Airbnb's experiences feature. You can earn more money by doing this and use your property as a venue. For example, you could host a cooking class or a fun activity such as a scavenger hunt around your neighborhood. People love these off-the-beaten-path experiences and you can use it to push your listing higher in the search results.

Reviews

There's no denying it, reviews are all important on the internet. When starting out, it's going to be tough to get people to click on your listing. A good way of getting reviews is to offer people heavily discounted rates and request them to leave you a review on the platform. You can offer them stays of a night or two to collect reviews.

Consider asking your friends and family to book your place through the platform and leave a review. This will push your listing up the search results and you'll start to see more clicks. Once people start booking with you, request that they leave you a review. Don't hound them if they leave you a bad review. That's the easiest way to ensure no one ever stays with you again.

Often, you'll find that people who know your past guests will contact you directly to book your place. This is a very good sign and it shows that the word-of-mouth reviews of your place are great.

Convenience

Most people booking on Airbnb are on vacation. To this end, make it as hassle-free for them as possible. This means leaving notes around your property regarding how to operate appliances, the wifi password, and so on. You can offer Netflix or other amenities as add-ons to delight them even more.

It's also a great idea to leave snacks and other eatables in the fridge. This is something that will hugely endear you to your guests. Often, people arrive at unearthly hours and finding a snack waiting for them is a great gesture. You don't need to go overboard with this. A few crisps, bread, butter, and some fruits go a long way towards enhancing the homeliness of your place. Leaving them something to drink is also a great idea.

Greeting your guests when they arrive is the best option but this might not always be practical for you. Some people wish to be greeted and have a ton of questions. Some just want to be left alone. Be sensitive to their needs and act accordingly. Leave notes or a pamphlet informing them of everything they can do around the area as well.

If they're driving to your property, let them know of parking restrictions and anything else they ought to know a week before they arrive. This is a good way of personalizing your message and endearing you to them even more.

WHAT TO WATCH OUT FOR

There are a few disadvantages of using Airbnb as a means of earning money. For starters, you'll need to have some money set aside for advertising. You'll have a high turnover of people and this means arranging cleaning and preparing the apartment for the next guest needs to be efficient. Often, bad reviews are caused when the property is dirty or if cleaning doesn't take place as promised.

You should also check whether your landlord is fine with you running a rent-to-rent using Airbnb. Airbnb has a reputation of attracting people who are looking to use a place for a night or two and then moving on. You'll have the occasional tenant that doesn't respect your property and leaves it in an extremely dirty state.

The neighbors might object to the noise your tenants cause and there's no way of holding the tenants responsible since they'll move on after a day or two. Therefore, screening tenants is extremely important but you don't have much time to do this. Airbnb offers a tenant review system so you should check their reviews. However, it often comes down to guesswork and emotional feel. It's a risk that you'll have to contend with when running a business through Airbnb.

So always check whether the neighbors are okay with you renting your apartment through Airbnb. If they object, then don't tell your guests that they need to be quiet or discreet. Remember they're on a vacation so you don't want to give the impression that things aren't above board.

Running an Airbnb is the best way of making the greatest profit via a rent-to-rent strategy. So use it well and follow the previous tips. You'll end up making a lot of money and can scale your business easily.

8
BULK BUYING

Bulk buying is often clubbed together with buying off-plan properties but this isn't necessarily true. Bulk buys are a strategy that makes sense if you have prior investment experience and have the capital to pull off such a strategy. It's a pretty simple one. Bulk buyers buy property at discounted prices because they buy a lot of inventory upfront.

Typical properties that are bought in bulk include off-plan properties or bank-owned properties. The latter is an example of investing in distressed situations and can get hairy if you don't know what you're doing. Off-plan properties have a high degree of risk as I've already explained. In short, bulk buying will supercharge your returns but they'll also increase your risks.

Let's look at some of the most important factors that surround bulk buys.

FACTORS TO CONSIDER

The good news is you've already learned of all the factors you need to consider before entering a bulk buy situation. The bad news is you'll have to evaluate all of them for multiple properties, on a constrained timeline. Things like location and exit strategies are obvious. Your properties' location needs to be great and you should be crystal clear about your exit strategy.

However, much like buying toothpaste in bulk, there's a good chance that you'll be stuck with your properties for a while. If the market goes against you, you'll need to revamp your exit strategy. Then there's financing.

Financing

Financing bulk buys is much like finding money to fund property development. For starters, most bulk sellers won't negotiate bulk buys with individuals, unless you happen to have a great track record and are well known to the seller. For example, banks are great sources of bulk buys. However, for record keeping and audit purposes, banks rarely sell properties in bulk to a single buyer. This is because they'll usually offer financing with these properties and the risk of a single person buying them is too high.

Therefore, the best approach is to form a PLC and use that structure to source bulk buys. You'll be taken as a serious property developer even if your track record is full of single lets and smaller HMOs. Forming a company means sourcing financing is going to be tough. You have two options here.

You could either raise equity in your business by selling shares to investors or you could source debt through private investors or from lenders using a mortgage broker. Remember, you're looking for greater levels of financing so you might find that finding a balance between equity and debt makes more sense.

Some lenders specialize in lending to bulk buyers but approaching them without much of a track record of bulk buys or a relationship is tough. Therefore, it's best to use a mortgage broker's services. It'll cost you money but it's worth the expense. It's best to develop a property before choosing to enter the bulk buying field. Credibility is extremely important for lenders so establish this before going the bulk buying route.

Taxes

Tax laws in the UK surrounding property investment have changed quite a bit over the past few years. Previously, landlords could claim mortgage interest as a deduction in their tax returns but this has been replaced with a 20% credit instead. While single let landlords have suffered because of this, bulk buyers have been hit harder.

What's more, lending criteria have also tightened with the government mandating more stringent affordability checks on property deals (Duncan, 2020). Then there's the stamp duty charge which works out to three percent of the overall property's value. The result is that property investment has become far less profitable for most landlords.

It's not all bad news though. The Multiple Dwellings Relief (MDR) clause is a bulk buyer's saviour. You can reduce your tax bill since under MDR rules, stamp duty land tax and the land transaction tax is levied on the average price you paid for your property portfolio. The law specifies that residential tax rates (including supplementary charges) be used to determine how much a landlord needs to pay. In Scotland, you won't pay the supplementary charge at all. Therefore, landlords in England, Wales, and Northern Ireland need to choose between paying stamp duty on the average property price or on individual property prices at lower tax rates. While the rates might be lower, keep in mind that the amounts paid might be higher, depending on your choice.

While most bulk buyers use corporations to buy properties, it's best to consult a tax adviser before doing so. If your aim is to build a large portfolio, then the ability to write off interest payments against earnings is invaluable. You'll also pay taxes at lower corporation rates. However, if you're looking to move existing property holdings into a company structure, you might incur additional stamp duty and capital gains charges (potentially).

There's also the question of whether you wish to withdraw all of your rental profits. Corporations pay a flat rate of 19% while individuals pay 45% taxes. That's quite a substantial difference! However, this lower tax rate is offset against HMRC's treatment of property investments at the end of your life.

Since they're held by a business, properties are not excepted from inheritance taxes on your death. Your heirs will incur a 40% tax liability which will probably force them to sell the property in a hurry. It's best to speak to a tax advisor to figure out the best structure for your operations. With bulk purchases, the individual issues with property investing get amplified since your portfolio is that much larger.

ADVANTAGES AND DISADVANTAGES

There are a few advantages to bulk property purchases. The most apparent one is the ability to generate a significant return on your investment. When you buy properties in bulk, you'll receive a discount from the seller. Bulk buyers are typically welcomed by the organizations that sell them. For example, unsold properties burn a hold in a bank's pocket.

Their business is collecting interest on properties, not running them as landlords. Therefore, anyone who can step in and relieve them of their burden will receive significant incentives to do so. A property developer will welcome off-plan bulk buyers with open arms because it allows them to quickly offload properties and generate the cash they need to reduce their financing burden.

The discount you'll receive will allow you to earn a huge profit when you sell your properties. The flip side is that buying in bulk always means greater risks. If the property market turns against you, you'll be stuck with a portfolio of properties that aren't earning you money.

There's also the fact that your exit strategies might be compromised. Instead of selling properties, you might be forced to become a landlord. It's impossible to landlord all of your properties and you'll need to hire a property management firm to do this for you. This means more expenses and you might not have accounted for all of them.

At the end of the day, bulk buying property is a great strategy. The key is to carefully evaluate all of your options and work the numbers out ahead of time. Consult with tax professionals before you decide to put your strategies into action and prepare for the worst case scenario.

9

NEGOTIATING THE BEST DEALS

When it comes down to it, real estate is all about negotiation. How well you negotiate goes a long way towards determining the quality of your relationships with people who will support your business, as well as the overall profits you can earn. I'm not saying that someone who negotiates well is going to earn gargantuan profits compared to someone who doesn't.

However, a good negotiator will source better deals on the market since the best ones tend to get snapped up before they're advertised. Negotiation is all about creating trust with someone else and forming a relationship. Most people approach it as a task where one seeks to outsmart the other but this approach never pays dividends. You might bulldoze your way forward with a few deals but, at the end of the day, you're not going to make much progress.

NEGOTIATION TIPS

At a basic level, all of us know how to negotiate. The topic tends to get over complicated by salesy types who try to convince everyone else that they're smarter than the rest. This isn't true. Sure, there are a few technicalities that you should watch out for but these are easily learned. The best tip

I can give you is to always be considerate but stick to your boundaries.

Plan

Many beginner real estate investors make a huge mistake before negotiations even begin. They fail to plan. You should know your maths by heart before you enter negotiations. You should have mapped out different scenarios beforehand, roughly speaking. This is because the seller is going to offer you different prices and you need to know how that affects you.

There's also the fact that you can ask the seller to cover some of your costs and this makes a big difference to your bottom line. If the property needs a few repairs, you could request them to do it for you and increase your bid. There are many moving parts to a negotiation so don't think you should have everything worked out ahead of time.

Instead, focus on understanding the picture roughly before you begin. This will help you to manage expectations and give you good grounding to negotiate from. Lastly, you'll make a good impression on the seller because you'll clearly come across as someone who has prepared and is a serious investor.

Emotional Control

People who are new to negotiation tend to lose their rag when things don't go their way. You will encounter situations where you'll go in expecting one thing but receive something else entirely. This is normal. Don't lose your head and accuse the seller of being underhanded. Remember that you can always walk away.

Often, you'll see a property that poses a great investment opportunity and you'll begin building your expectations up by thinking of the profits you could earn. However, these expectations also work against you if the situation goes against you. Don't lash out or get too disappointed if this happens.

Remember that no piece of property is so valuable so as to lose your calm over it. There will always be other properties and opportunities. Draw your boundaries and stick to them politely but resolutely. I'm not saying you should never be flexible. However, it's best to allow some wiggle room and not get too emotionally attached to the opportunity.

Be Direct

Is something on your mind? Say it! Do you want the seller to do something for you? Request it! Many beginners beat around the bush in the hopes that the seller can read their minds and spare them perceived embarrassment. This is a waste of everyone's time. Instead, be direct and clearly communicate what you want.

Know When to Walk Away

This tip is tied to controlling your emotions. Every once in a while, you'll encounter a delusional seller who thinks their property is a gift from the Almighty. In such situations, negotiation is a hopeless task. A great property that comes attached with a seller that is uninterested in a win-win situation is not worth spending your time on.

Feel free to walk away. In every negotiation, all parties insinuate their willingness to walk away but not everyone is willing to do so. Actually, walking away is a powerful tactic and sends the message that you know what you're doing. It makes the other party perk up and realize that they can't bulldoze their way through a deal.

Seek Help

Trying to do everything by themselves and not seeking help is a common mistake that beginners make. When you enter deal negotiations, seek as much help as possible from other real estate professionals. If this means bringing an agent along to help you unearth problems, or asking a tradesperson to help you spot issues, do it. Yes, it will cost you most but think of it as an investment.

The money these professionals will save you will be greater than what you pay them. Avoid being penny-wise but pound-foolish. If you find that you can't afford to seek help, then you're under-capitalized and need to focus on raising more money. Don't enter a negotiation without enough capital or without adequate support.

You'll place yourself in a weak position right from the beginning and you're unlikely to get what you want.

Be Cheerful

This tip will help you more than anything else. Property negotiations can get you down. You'll mention a bid price and the seller counters with something else. The dance can get weary after a while and it might tire you. As silly as it might seem sometimes, remember why you're in this. Remember the promise that real estate investment holds for you and your future. This will put you in a better mood instantly.

Negotiating when irritated or annoyed is the easiest way to put the seller off you and you're unlikely to get what you want. You shouldn't come across as fake, either. Don't try to become an expert on the seller's niece's university problems or some obscure facet of their lives. Keep it professional, be cheerful, and know that you have the ability to walk away and find even better deals at all times.

Negotiate Everything

Remember that, in a real estate deal, almost everything is negotiable. You won't find the seller's boundaries unless you make an effort to discover them. You shouldn't be the annoying person who asks for unreasonable things but you should also avoid being too timid. Ask the seller about repairs and other things they could help you with.

A common mistake that prospective buyers make is to paint everything negatively. If a fence needs repairs, don't point it out and call it broken down or worn out. Instead, politely ask the seller whether they're willing to spruce it up or carry out repairs. The seller knows what needs repair without you pointing it out to them.

You'll often encounter sellers who have lived in their properties their entire lives. There are real memories associated with every part of their home. Tread carefully and be positive at all times. Don't slag anything off in an attempt to drive prices lower. You'll only end up being shown the door if you do this.

CONCLUSION

Property investment is one of the best ways of building wealth in the UK. The stock market might seem like a great place to park your money but there are significant barriers you'll face. First, the stock market is extremely volatile and who knows when some bank is going to detonate the economy anyway?

The other problem with stocks is that you cannot use leverage to boost your returns in a scalable and safe way. With real estate, the ability to borrow money safely and control a large amount of assets is invaluable. There is a fully fleshed out network and support system that allows you to do this. As a result, you can boost your wealth efficiently, without assuming too much risk.

Note that risk is always present, no matter what the opportunity looks like. The key to successful investing is to mitigate your risks at all times and prepare for worst-case scenarios. In real estate investing, you should always prepare for the market to turn against you or for your exit strategy to hit a snag. Don't panic. Instead, enter a deal with the expectation that something will go pear shaped.

This will put you in a problem-solving frame of mind and you'll tide over issues easily. Real estate investing is extremely rewarding when done right but you have to choose the right strategy. What is right for one person might not work for you. Study all of the strategies listed in this book thoroughly and match them to your psyche. Remember that there isn't a "best" strategy out there. It all depends on your comfort level.

Never become emotionally attached to a property as I've explained previously. Getting emotional over a property is only going to result in you overpaying for or overestimating its strengths and ignoring its weaknesses. At the end of the day, the properties you'll be investing in aren't your home. They're there to make you money. Treat them accordingly.

If you choose to become a landlord, draw clear boundaries with your tenants and always enforce your rules. Do not become emotionally attached to them or start to think of them as being your closest friends. You won't be able to enforce your rules and you'll get taken advantage of. I'm not saying your tenants will be malicious. It's just that your tenants don't own your property and will naturally be less careful with it than you will.

Throughout your property investment journey you will have the chance to work with professionals in the business. Don't be shy of asking questions of them and don't penny pinch when paying for their services. Always seek help and you'll end up making more money. I'm not saying that you should use them as a crutch. However, be honest about your shortcomings and seek help with the things that you need clarification with.

This book is the beginning of your property investment journey and I hope you're as excited as I am! I'm positive that the strategies you've learned here will help you achieve prosperity. Let me know what you think by leaving me a review.

Here's wishing you all the prosperity and riches on your investing journey!

REFERENCES

Anatomy of a property hotspot—12 indicators. (2021, March 3). Www.propertytribes.com. https://www.propertytribes.com/anatomy-of-a-property-hotspot-12-indicators-t-127624795.html

Babaee, A. (2020). What is a bridging loan? Money.co.uk. https://www.money.co.uk/bridging-loans/what-is-a-bridging-loan.htm

Duncan, E. (2020). How should landlords with multiple properties deal with the tax issues? Financial Times. https://www.ftadviser.com/property/2020/01/30/how-should-landlords-with-multiple-properties-deal-with-the-tax-issues/

Flipping property. (2018, August 1). Addicted to Property. https://addictedtoproperty.co.uk/property-flipping/

HMO property investment | Ultimate guide. (2018, October 30). FJP Investment. https://www.fjpinvestment.co.uk/hmo-property-investment-ultimate-guide

Landlord tax changes: What are allowable expenses? (2021, March 3). Foxtons. https://www.foxtons.co.uk/discover/2017/03/landlord-tax-changes-what-are-allowable-expenses.html

Property maintenance costs: How not to blow your budget. (2019, August 1). No Letting Go Inventory Management. https://nolettinggo.co.uk/blog/property-maintenance-costs/

Reassignments—what actually are they? (2020). LiFE Residential. https://liferesidential.co.uk/news/reassignments-what-actually-are-they/

Where to invest in a buy-to-let property to get the best return. (2021, March 3). Moneytothemasses.com. https://moneytothemasses.com/saving-for-your-future/buy-to-lets/where-to-invest-in-a-buy-to-let-property-to-get-the-best-returns

Why should you invest in UK property? (2021, March 3). SevenCapital. https://sevencapital.com/uk-property-investment/why-invest-in-uk-property/